The Ultimate Reiki Guide for Practitioners and Masters

Lawrence Ellyard

Author of 'Reiki Healer'
Founder of the International Institute for Reiki Training

www.reikitraining.com.au

BOOKS

Winchester, U.K.
New York, U.S.A.

First published by O Books, 2006
An imprint of John Hunt Publishing Ltd., The Bothy, Deershot
Lodge, Park Lane, Ropley, Hants, SO24 0BE, UK
office@johnhunt-publishing.com
www.o-books.net

USA and Canada
NBN
custserv@nbnbooks.com
Tel: 1 800 462 6420
Fax: 1 800 338 4550

Singapore
STP
davidbuckland@tlp.com.sg
Tel: 65 6276
Fax: 65 6276 7119

Australia
Brumby Books
sales@brumbybooks.com
Tel: 61 3 9761 5535
Fax: 61 3 9761 7095

South Africa
Alternative Books
altbook@global.co.za
Tel: 27 011 792 7730
Fax: 27 011 972 7787

New Zealand
Peaceful Living
books@peaceful-living.co.nz
Tel: 64 09 921 6222
Fax: 64 09 921 6220

Text copyright Lawrence Ellyard 2006
Design: Jim Weaver Design, Basingstoke
Cover design: Infograf Ltd, London

ISBN 1 905047 48 7

A CIP catalogue record for this book is available from the British
Library.

Printed by Maple-Vail, USA

Contents

Author's note

The Ultimate Reiki Guide for Practitioners and Masters is essentially divided into two sections. Section One (*Reiki for a Living*) guides new and established Reiki Practitioners in the practice of Reiki, details what it takes to establish your Reiki practice; and discusses effective marketing of your practice, to reach people who will benefit from the valuable service you offer.

Section Two (*Reiki Sensei*) is a guide to the art of teaching Reiki. Whether you are already a teacher of Reiki or intend to begin this journey, you will find a valuable source of information and methods for passing on the Usui system of natural healing.

In *Reiki: 200 Q&A for Beginners*, the emphasis takes the reader through an overview of the Reiki system, encountering the common and not so commonly asked questions about Reiki.

This book takes our journey a step further, going into the practice of Reiki for more experienced practitioners and teachers of Reiki.

Introduction

Since the early 1970's when Reiki was first introduced to the United States, Reiki's popularity has received increasing popularity. From only a handful of teachers, today Reiki has grown world-wide to practitioner numbers in the millions. Reiki teaches effective methods for self-healing and healing others as well as practices for spiritual development, yet few Reiki practitioners have any understanding of how to promote themselves so that their gifts may be shared with others.

The Ultimate Reiki Guide for Practitioners and Masters not only offers down to earth advice on giving Reiki treatments, it also offers much needed practical information on how to reach as many people as possible with Reiki and still manage to pay the bills at the end of the day.

All of the advice outlined throughout Part One can be utilized by any healthcare practitioner with exceptional results. These tried and tested tools for marketing one's business not only work well, they guarantee an increase in both clientele and one's profit margin.

In Part Two of this book, you will find all the advice you need to become a confident teacher of Reiki. You'll learn how to run your own Reiki classes with all the practical skills needed to teach and embody the spiritual path of Reiki.

Whether you are a seasoned Reiki practitioner, teacher or just beginning, *The Ultimate Reiki Guide for Practitioners and Masters* will show you how to truly walk the path of Reiki with humility, healing and wisdom.

Throughout Section 1 you will learn:
- Practical advice for giving Reiki treatments from start to finish, including how to give Reiki treatments in a home or office setting.
- How to give a Reiki treatment in the Western style, as well as how to treat others using Japanese healing techniques.
- How to create value to your practice, including the "rules" of

ethical practice, getting paid and nurturing the practitioner/client relationship.
- How to handle enquiries and how to make the most out of the internet.
- How to effectively promote yourself, how to gain free publicity and get known in the Reiki industry.
- How to expand your client base and develop enticing offers that will dramatically increase your clientele, as well as discovering the winning secrets of success.

Throughout Section 2 you will learn:
- The pre-requisites to becoming a Reiki teacher.
- How to effectively teach Reiki classes.
- Advice on being a teacher and serving an apprenticeship.
- The truth about some common Reiki Myths.
- Tips for giving Reiki Attunements and personal development.
- How to walk the Spiritual path with Reiki.
- How to create a sacred space for teaching.
- How to create Reiki Manuals and Certificates.
- How to cultivate true Reiki Mastery.

How to use this book
The Reiki Guide is set out as a reference book. Although this book is designed to be read from cover to cover, you can determine which areas concern you most. If you already have experience in the practice of Reiki but are not sure how to set up a practice, you can skip ahead to the next relevant section. Throughout this book various exercises are set out at the end of some chapters, enabling you to put your practice into affirmative action.

It is my hope that this book will take your practice through new unchartered waters, and by using the guidelines presented, you will arrive at a destination of health, humility and healing.

Yours in Reiki
Lawrence Ellyard

Section One
Reiki for a Living

1
All About Reiki

Reiki History – A brief overview

Compared to many healing traditions, Reiki is a considerably new system, founded in the early part of the 20th Century by a Japanese Buddhist named Mikao Usui. Although Mikao Usui was primarily a Buddhist, he also studied many of the religious systems of his day including Christianity which was brought to Japan by the first Western Missionaries. Over several years, Mikao Usui refined his system of healing and in the last years before his death in 1926, he had trained some 2000 people in the art of Reiki. In turn, many of his students went on to teach, passing on the Usui system to their own students. Reiki continued to be passed from teacher to student until the present day, albeit branching out into several new styles. As the teachings of Reiki were passed on in an oral tradition, today many facts concerning the origins of Reiki and the life of Mikao Usui remain largely unknown. What is known is largely based on anecdotal research gathered from his former students and a translation of his memorial stone, which was erected by his students shortly after his death in 1926[*].

Reiki Today

Mikao Usui left a legacy which has today become a world-wide success. With the enormous popularity and user-friendly nature of Reiki, this system has now been taught to millions of people world-wide.

Curiously, however, what many people do not understand is that not

---

[*] For a comprehensive account of the history of Reiki see chapter 3 in *Reiki: 200 Q&A for Beginners*.

all forms of Reiki are the same. With the sheer number of teachers and due to the oral tradition by which Reiki was first promulgated in the United States, perhaps Reiki can be more likened to a great 'Chinese Whisper'. In the Takata (Western) style, this oral tradition prevented the use of written manuals, so students and teachers had to rely solely on their memory. As a result, in a few short years, the system became more and more fragmented.

Added to this were the many teachers who added or removed aspects of the system, making it their own. Inevitably, this left the Reiki teachings somewhat altered from their original form, and so today it becomes harder and harder to find an authentic Reiki lineage.

Fortunately in the early 1990's, further discoveries of the original Reiki teachings were found. Usui's memorial was discovered and many of Reiki's missing links were uncovered. Further revelations included the discovery of a living Reiki tradition in Japan with additional methods as taught by the Reiki Gakkai *(Japans Reiki Learning Society)*. Further to this, a number of Usui's notes and manuals were also recovered and this lead to even greater revelations. These discoveries were later made available and for the first time, western teachers of Reiki gained new information regarding the original Japanese system. This information did much to piece together some of the "lost" Reiki teachings.

Based on these new discoveries, much of the way Reiki has been taught in the past has now changed. Much like an archaeological find, these fragments from the past can tell us a great deal about Reiki today.

What is Reiki?

Reiki is a method of hands-on healing which originated in Japan at the turn of the 20th Century. It is a system of healing that transforms and heals the body and mind. Utilizing the methods within the Reiki system, the Reiki practitioner transfers healing energy via the hands to another.

Reiki energy is the healing energy of the Universe. It represents a matrix of non-dualistic energy, which permeates all things. A Reiki practitioner harnesses this vital energy via a series of attunements which, in effect, switch on the ability to transfer Reiki energy to oneself and others.

The transmission of this energy comes via a Reiki teacher, someone who knows the precise methods for creating this alignment within a practitioner. Once this alignment is complete, the practitioner can then use this healing energy in a variety of ways to restore the body, mind and emotions into a harmonious state.

Reiki has beneficial results for those who give, as well as those who receive it. It creates an avenue for healing which includes healing the primary cause of illness as well as its physical manifestations.

Reiki Attunements

The Reiki attunements are the energy alignments a teacher of Reiki gives to a student. In various schools and styles of Reiki, the way these attunements are given to the student vary in approach and methodology. However, irrespective of differences in methodology, in most cases each attunement activates an ability to use Reiki energy for oneself and others, almost immediately.

If we were to use an analogy of what an attunement is, then we might think the Reiki energy is a radio signal; our body a radio; and our radio antenna or receiver the body's energy system. When a teacher adjusts our antenna by tuning in our dials, or Chakras, we effectively pick up the station 'Reiki' and as a result, any previous static that was found on our station is removed and a clear reception is found. Thus the ability to channel Reiki energy is bestowed.

Another amazing thing about this system is that one need not believe in Reiki for it to work. Thus, ruling out a placebo effect, the Reiki healing ability can be successfully bestowed on anyone.

The actual Reiki attunement is a short ceremony, which creates this alignment. Many attunement procedures make use of symbols particular to the system and these are drawn by the teacher into various places of energy flow in the recipient's body. The symbols act like keys. Much like opening a door, these symbols open new pathways of energy, which previously lay dormant or 'locked up' in an individuals energy system.

Reiki Lineage

A Reiki lineage describes the family tree of Reiki teachers and their students', dating back to the founder, Mikao Usui. A Reiki lineage is much like an ancestry of those who have previously walked the path of Reiki.

To illustrate an example, one well-known Reiki lineage is that of Mrs. Takata, who was responsible for bringing Reiki to the west for the very first time. Her Lineage, or family tree goes like this: Usui, Hayashi, Takata.

Hayashi was a student of Usui. Hayashi became a teacher in his own right and in time began to teach his own students. One of his students was Mrs. Takata, who received the attunements into Reiki and finally became a teacher in her own right. She in turn began to teach her own students, some of whom became teachers of her system. And so the lineage grows, with each generation of teacher.

There are, of course, many other Reiki Lineages, some are many teachers' long and some of the methods *(depending upon the teachers in those lineages)* have changed or adapted the Reiki teachings. Subsequently, information may change from teacher to teacher and as a consequence, the transmission may weaken. On the other hand, there are some Reiki lineages which have remained unchanged over many decades in Japan, giving students the opportunity to learn a more traditional and original Reiki style.

When a student receives a Reiki attunement, a connection to the lineage of the Reiki teacher is conferred. The student's Reiki lineage is in place from that point on. One then usually inherits the teachings and transmission of this lineage with instruction via their teacher.

A Reiki teacher or, as often described, a *'Reiki Master'*, has the ability to give a transmission and to pass on the lineage of their teachers' tradition. A Reiki practitioner, on the other hand, can give Reiki to others, but cannot pass on the Reiki transmission.

2

How to give a Reiki Treatment

Interviewing the Client

Once you have made initial contact, be this over the telephone, via email or in person and have arranged a suitable time to give a Reiki treatment, there are a number of factors which should be considered.

One of the things to remember is that you are there to assist this person in the best way possible, therefore you need to ask them what they need in terms of their healing.

The following are some standard questions which should be asked prior to treatment:

- Have you received a Reiki Treatment before and if so when?
- What was the nature of the treatment and your complaint at that time?
- How are you currently feeling?
- Is there anything or any specific area where you require healing?

For mental and emotional issues, ask your client to locate where they feel the disturbing emotion resides. If they are unable to determine this, you can help them by guiding them through a short focussing exercise to ascertain the physical location of the emotional imbalance.

An example might be:

> Practitioner: *How are you feeling?*
> Client: *Not very well, I've been feeling down and depressed.*
> Practitioner: *If this feeling of depression resided somewhere in your body, where would it be?*
> Client: *Not sure.*
> Practitioner: *Close your eyes and tune into the feeling of depression*

or imagine the last time you felt depressed. Now tune into this feeling and your body. If it had a place, where would it reside in your body?
Client: *Feels like a heavy feeling in my solar plexus.*

This is an example of how you might determine the origin of an emotional issue. From this place you can begin your treatment with hands-on healing.

Building Rapport

Once you have established what your client needs in terms of their healing, it is ideal to be sympathetic to their situation. You might recall an experience that you had similar to their situation or an experience of another *(provided this does not break client confidentiality)*.

Make and maintain eye contact with your client and allow yourself to be open to not only hearing their situation, but being aware of their body language and overall tone of communication. One can readily observe many subtle signs of body language when speaking with a client for the first time. Through observation, mindfulness and focused awareness you will be able to perceive how best to serve your new client in the treatment which follows.

Client Comfort

Now that you have determined what is necessary for the client's needs, you want to make the treatment as comfortable as possible for them. They are receiving Reiki to be nurtured and healed, both physically and mentally, so preparing a space which is conducive to healing is paramount.

Check that your client is lying comfortably and has adequate warmth or will not become overly hot during the session. In colder climates, it is always suggested to have a blanket handy and to have a well heated room, as it is often the case that a person's body temperature will decrease during a Reiki treatment.

In the summer months, when the outside temperature can be either humid or overly hot, a light breeze from a fan or open window can be enough to maintain a comfortable temperature. In hot climates where one is using air conditioning, it pays to always keep a blanket handy and be aware not to overly cool the room to an uncomfortable chill.

A light blanket covering your client's body can also add a sense of security and safety in their mind during the treatment.

Pillows are another comfort factor. Check that the pillow is at a comfortable height that suits your clients' needs. Some people prefer a very low pillow or none at all, whereas some clients like two pillows under their head. Don't assume that your client will like what you like, therefore it is worth checking this.

If the client is lying on their back, a pillow or bolster under their knees can also assist the lower back from any strain that might otherwise come from lying in one position for an extended period of time.

In terms of lighting, it is suggested that the lighting be subdued in order to create a soothing ambience.

To relate a personal experience, I once received a Reiki treatment in an office space where two flourescent lights were flickering intermittently directly above my head. Even with my eyes closed, I could not only hear the buzzing sound, but could see the flashes from the lights from behind my eyelids. Needless to say, it was not the most comfortable environment to receive a treatment. Although it would have been correct to say something, I decided to suffer in silence. More often than not we have been brought up to be polite and not to say anything which might otherwise disturb us during a session so as not to hurt the practitioner's feelings. Recipients of Reiki will often lay there for an hour, quietly suffering as something continually annoys them.

So it is important to ask your client, *are you comfortable*, thus giving them the opportunity to let you know what would better serve their level of comfort during the treatment.

Before the Treatment

Before you commence a Reiki treatment there are some other recommended pointers worth mentioning:

- Demonstrate for the recipient some hand positions that you will be using during the treatment on your own body.
- Ask about the condition of the recipient's body, any disorders, current injury, previous surgery, or current medication, and what their goals are for the Reiki treatment.
- Do not remove clothing (recipient or practitioner) unless it is to

loosen a belt, or remove a tie or shoes. You might also ask your client
to remove bulky jewellery or loosen tight garments.
- Because of the often close proximity of yourself to your client, be sure
that you have washed your hands prior to treatment and that your
breath is fresh.
- Place a pillow under the recipient's knees and head (for their comfort).
- Keep a box of tissues handy in the event that your client experiences
an emotional release or simply needs to blow their nose.
- Never promise a healing. You can tell someone Reiki will balance
and relax the body, and may relieve pain and symptoms. It is not our
role to play Doctor.

During the Treatment

- There are several basic hand positions for a traditional treatment.
Hold each for five or more minutes, or until your hands feel like they
need to move. If you are applying Reiki on an intuitive level, then
apply the hands for as long as you feel is necessary.
- Keep your fingers and thumb together. Open fingers creates a
dispersed energy, while closed fingers creates a focussed energy.
- Your hands may feel different sensations: heat, cold, tingling, pulling,
etc. Hands may not get hot. Do not judge the effectiveness – the Reiki
energy is working.
- Soft and gentle music can also be good during a treatment. Be sure to
determine what soothing music your client likes.
- It is not necessary to be in a meditative state during a treatment to
achieve beneficial results, although you will often experience these
states with practice.
- Talking during treatments is permitted, but silence enhances your
awareness of energy in the client's body. In some cases talking can
have a cleansing effect for your client.
- When your client is asleep, the energy seems to be more readily
accepted (as there is no resistance from the conscious mind). If your
client falls asleep, do not become overly concerned, the energy is
giving them space for rest.
- Reiki adjusts to the needs and conditions of the receiver, so your
experience may be that the energy feels different, depending on the
hand position and person being treated.

After the Treatment

- Rinse your hands and even your forearms in cold water (this breaks contact with the person's energy field and assists in clearing any unwanted energy.)
- Both you and the recipient should drink some water as this assists any detoxifying as a result of the treatment.
- If you have facilitated treatments during the day, take a shower in the evening to clean the excess energy from your aura and practice the self-cleansing exercises. It is also advisable to change your clothing as unwanted energy can become embedded within your clothes.

Things to Remember

- Remember you are not the healer – Reiki is.
- If the person does not seem to get better, take comfort that the Reiki energy is working on levels other than physical.
- For accidents and medical emergencies – ALWAYS APPLY FIRST AID FIRST and call for medical assistance where needed. Once you have attended to the client's needs you may wish to treat local areas (to reduce bleeding, shock or stress) then if possible, treat other positions.
- It is quite okay to only apply Reiki to 3 or 4 positions during a 1 hour treatment where the area of injury or illness may require additional time to heal.
- Never treat a child alone; always have a parent or guardian present.
- Do not diagnose or prescribe anything, unless you are licensed to do so.
- Reiki works on all levels. It covers the circulatory and endocrine systems, all major organs and the major Chakras *(energy centres)* of the body.
- Both hands channel Reiki equally. It is not necessary to consider the positive or negative sides of the body for hand placement. Reiki is a non-dualistic energy.
- Reiki is not just for when you are sick, so remember to give yourself Reiki on a daily basis.
- A little Reiki is better than no Reiki at all. Use your Reiki when you have a hand free. Informal healing like this can do much for your own peace of mind and calm you during the day.
- You cannot wear out Reiki – it is unlimited, just like you.

Practitioners Tips – Hygiene

It should be obvious to many but you may be surprised just how many times you might encounter some of the following breaches in hygiene:

Practitioners should wash their hands both before and after a treatment, especially if you have been preparing food or if you are a smoker. In every case, your hands should be thoroughly clean.

It is also advisable to avoid eating strong smelling foods such as garlic and onions prior to giving a treatment. In any case, brush your teeth prior to giving a treatment or gargle with mouthwash.

On the subject of smelly things, also be mindful of your armpits and feet. There can be nothing more off-putting than to endure your practitioner's armpits in your face or the smell of sweaty feet wafting up to your nasal level during a treatment. The idea is that your client should be aided in their own healing and relaxation during a session, so we should not add to their discomfort through lacking awareness in the nasal department.

Another point is your overall presentation. It is not advisable to be dressed in flowing white robes, nor should we look overly scruffy. Our presentation should be neat and clean with attention to our nails and hair being well groomed.

It is also advisable to have some tissues handy for ladies whose makeup and lipstick might be smeared when lying face down on the pillow or covers. It is also useful when treating the face positions where your hands may become overly sweaty as a result of the transference of Reiki energy. So a tissue over the eyes can aid in preventing spoiling makeup.

The last point is the treatment table covers, blankets and pillow slips. These should be frequently cleaned and pressed, presenting a fresh and welcoming appearance.

Types of Reiki Treatment

In the following chapter on Reiki techniques, we will discuss several ways to give a Reiki treatment from both the more common Western and less known Eastern styles of Reiki. Whether the practitioner is utilizing a set sequence of hand positions and systematically treating the whole of the body or working intuitively, it is important to remain open to what you may sense and feel during a treatment and not use the time to *'go off with the fairies'*. Giving Reiki to another is also an opportunity to train your mind in awareness, so be mindful of your thoughts during the treatment.

3
Reiki Techniques

Traditional Hand Positions

In the Western style of Reiki, a sequence for applying the hands upon another person is generally the format for most treatments. This is in order to cover the major areas of energy flow, as well as energizing the major organs and energy centres of the body. This system of hand positions was introduced to the original Reiki teachings initially by Hayashi and later adapted slightly by Mrs. Takata

The Hayashi/Takata systematic hands-on healing approach works on the premise of twelve positions on the front of the body and twelve positions on the back of the body. (Schools vary in this approach).

The hand positions are a way to facilitate a general healing and to boost the life force and vitality of the recipient. The hands are usually left in these positions from three to five minutes, with the whole session taking approximately one, to one and a half hours.

Short Reiki Treatment (Seated)

In you do not have a treatment table or do not have time to give a full treatment, then a short seated treatment may be an alternative option. Here the recipient is seated in a chair and the head, shoulders and front of the body are given the Reiki treatment. Although this method of treatment does not afford the recipient the chance to go deeper (falling asleep) the benefits are just as rewarding.

Full Reiki Treatment

When giving a full treatment it is worth considering an approach which will support your treatment. The following is a general guide to giving a Reiki treatment. Here we can identify four major stages:

Phase #1

The first phase is the introduction to the client, which includes determining where the client wishes to have Reiki and any areas of concern, as well as client comfort.

Phase #2

The second phase is where the practitioner mentally prepares to give the Reiki treatment. This includes a centring procedure, merging with the Reiki energy and performing an individual ritual process for centring and connecting with the Reiki energy.

Phase #3

The third phase is the administering of the Reiki treatment. This represents the bulk of the treatment time, when the practitioner administers Reiki to the areas in need or takes the systematic approach of treating all the major areas of the body in the form of the 12 treatment positions as recommended in the traditional Hayashi/Takata style of Reiki treatment.

Phase #4

The fourth phase is where the practitioner, having completed the treatment, disconnects from the client's energy field and closes the treatment. This may include certain cleansing and closing procedures, as a way to disconnect from the recipients energy field.

Finally, the client and the practitioner share their experiences. This may include where the Reiki energy seemed to draw the most energy and to determine whether further treatments are desired or are necessary. It is important to note that the practitioner does not interpret, diagnose, or prescribe in the closing phase.

The following is a more detailed approach to giving a Reiki treatment, which can be used by anyone, regardless of Reiki style.

Phase #1 The introduction to the client

Before you place your hands on someone, it is necessary to ascertain their needs for healing. One of the best ways to determine this is by asking your client the following questions:

1. Introduce yourself by name to the client.

2. Ask if they have received Reiki before. If they have, then proceed to step 4.
3. If they have not, take a moment to briefly describe what is involved. An example might be: *"Reiki is the transference of vital energy and what I am going to do is place my hands on your body in the areas which correspond to the major areas of energy flow, to boost your vital energy."*
4. Ask if they have any areas of concern? *"Do you have any areas which require healing on a physical, mental, or emotional level?"*
5. Once you have determined some areas of concern, ask them if they are sufficiently comfortable and whether they have any questions. Then ask them to relax and close their eyes.

Phase #2 Centring yourself

Now that you have determined your client's areas of need and have created a space for their comfort, you are ready to prepare yourself energetically for the treatment. We do this in the following manner:

1. Begin by placing your hands in the prayer Mudra *(hand gesture)* with hands folded at heart level. The intention is to merge with the Reiki energy in the following way. This establishes not only a connection, but an energetic protection throughout the treatment.
2. One makes the strong wish to benefit the person in a way which supports their healing. You may wish to affirm this by saying: *"May whatever healing energy transfers during this treatment be for this person's highest good, restoring their balance and wellness."*
3. Now extend your hands high above your head, reaching to connect to the fullness of the Reiki energy. *(You can imagine your body filling with energy).* One imagines touching a vast field of energy and light. You can also imagine this as being like an enormous planet, representing the unlimited power of Reiki. Once you have made this connection, slowly move your hands down the front of your body, with your palms facing you. In the same way water would fill a glass, imagine that as your hands descend, the Reiki energy is merging with your energy field and body. Your hands move to the sides of your body, fingers relaxed. Feel your breath flowing naturally and slowly and drop your awareness to your lower abdomen.
- Alternatively, one can simply imagine this merging happening without the outer form, keeping your hands folded at heart level, in the prayer Mudra.

Now that you have merged with the Reiki energy, you are ready to commence the healing treatment.

Phase #3 The healing treatment

The treatment time can be anywhere from 30 to 90 minutes, depending how much time is necessary. The healing treatment can be facilitated in the following manner:

1. Unless the client has advised a specific area of concern (which requires immediate attention), begin with the head positions. These first five positions assist the body in relaxing and aid the general flow of healing energy throughout the entire body.

The first five positions are as follows:

Position 1

Position 2

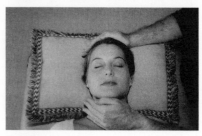

Position 3

Positions 4 and 5

Note: *positions #4 and #5 may be combined together.*

2. Be sure to ask your client just after you have initially placed your hands on them, to determine the level of touch. Ask them quietly: *"How is my touch, are my hands too heavy or too light?"* Then adjust your hands if necessary.
3. Spend a reasonable amount of time in each position, ideally at least three minutes for each position. This will give the Reiki energy a

chance to penetrate into the areas of concern, to optimise healing.
4. Allow the Reiki energy to guide you. Keep your hands on an area
    that feels most appropriate or the areas that you feel drawn to. This
    also includes the areas your client has requested. If they have an
    injury or place of illness, one should keep their hands on these areas
    for a longer period of time.
5. Keep your hands on this position until you feel a change in the
    energy. Once the area feels like it has had enough energy, move to
    the next position.
    *[NOTE: under no circumstances should you compromise the client's
    boundaries by placing your hands on or near the breasts, buttocks, or
    genital area. In cases where healing energy is required in these areas,
    place your hands a few inches above.]*
6. If you wish, employ visualization into your treatment. For example,
    one can imagine one is breathing in radiant healing energy through
    the crown and central channel and breathing out healing energy via
    the hands, into the client's body.
7. Be tender with your movements, thoughts and intent. Once you feel
    the healing is complete, you are ready to close the session. In most
    cases, finish your session on the feet, as this assists in grounding
    your client.

Phase #4 The closing procedure

1. Once you feel the client has received all the healing energy they
    require, return your hands back into the prayer position at the
    middle of your chest. In your own way, give thanks for the healing
    energy which has transferred and dedicate the merit of this practice
    for the benefit of all that lives.
2. Prayer of Dedication: *"May whatever merit that has been generated
    by this positive activity, be shared with all beings, for the benefit of all
    that lives."*
3. To disconnect from your client's energy field and to clear any lesser
    energies which may have accumulated throughout the treatment, do
    the following procedure:
    Imagine that you have a blue sphere in your mouth. Raise your hands
    in prayer Mudra to your mouth and blow through the palms of your
    hands three times with this healing energy. Think to yourself "this
    now disconnects me from this person's energy field and transforms
    all lower energies".

4. Now wash your hands under running water and focus on your out breath. Breathe out through the hands to discharge any unwanted energy.

Other suggestions

1. Always wash your hands before and in between treatments. This aids in proper hygiene as well as maintaining energetic clarity.
2. Never interpret your client's experience, nor give your interpretation of your own experience. One can simply say where one felt more energy and do not get into prescribing anything or diagnosing their condition.
3. Determine with the client whether further treatments are desired or needed.

Reiki and Chakra Healing

Another approach to giving a Reiki treatment is to give Reiki to the Chakras. The word Chakra *(Sanskrit),* Cakkhu *(Pali)* means: wheel, centre, eye, energy nexus within the subtle energy body. The Chakras are the basis of the energetic structure of a human being. These energy centres stem along a central axis tube *(central channel)* that runs from the crown Chakra to the base of the body.

The Chakras are a vital link to the totality of our being. Each centre represents the myriad aspects of who we are. Working with these sources of energy can assist in our personal growth, well-being and personal development.

Each Chakra vibrates at a specific frequency and is affected by light, colour and sound. The Chakras can be affected by any of these means, as well as other frequencies.

The Chakra system also corresponds to the endocrine system of the body. The endocrine system controls the hormonal balance within human beings. These hormones have a strong effect on our emotions as individuals.

In the case where one or many of our Chakras are out of balance, this will also affect our endocrine system and as a result, our emotional body. This is why the method of Chakra balancing can be very beneficial in balancing the body, mind and emotions.

There are many schools of thought about the Chakras. In this example we will illustrate the common model in most eastern spiritual traditions.

The Chakra System

1. The Base Chakra
The base Chakra is situated at the base of the body, at the perineum muscle. The base Chakra governs the supply of energy to the reproductive organs, the kidneys, the adrenal glands and spinal column. The base Chakra relates to our will to live, survival, procreation, family law, fight-flight response and our basic human instincts. The corresponding colour is red.

2. The Sacral Chakra (Hara Chakra)
This Chakra is situated three finger widths below the belly button and stems from the front and back of the central channel. It is related to emotions of sensuality and sexuality. The sacral is also related to our drive in the physical world and supplies our immune system and sexual organs with additional power. The sacral Chakra is the seat of our personal power. The corresponding colour is orange.

3. The Solar Plexus Chakra
The solar plexus Chakra is situated where the rib cage meets in the lower chest. Like the sacral Chakra, it protrudes from the front and back of the body. This Chakra is related to issues of personal power, self-esteem/self-image and our emotional selves. It is linked to the gall bladder, the digestive system and the pancreas. The corresponding colour is yellow.

4. The Heart Chakra
The heart Chakra is located in the centre of our chest and governs our ability to give and receive love. Here is the seat of compassion, giving, self-sacrifice and unconditional love. The heart Chakra governs the heart, the thymus gland, the circulatory system and lungs. The corresponding colour is green.

5. The Throat Chakra
The throat Chakra is located in the centre of the throat and protrudes from back and front of the neck. This centre governs communication

and our ability to speak our truth or to voice our opinions. The corresponding colour is blue.

6. The Brow Chakra

This Chakra is located at the centre of our brow, between our eyebrows and the original hairline. This Chakra protrudes from the front and back of the head and governs our intuition and intellect. It is the active centre of our imagination and our abilities of intuition, clairvoyance and psychic sensitivity. This Chakra also relates to our pituitary and pineal glands. The corresponding colour is indigo.

7. The Crown Chakra

The crown Chakra is located eight finger widths from the original hairline at the top and back of the head and is directly vertical to the tips of the ears when drawn upwards. The crown Chakra governs our attributes of spiritual potential and universal understanding. Other related factors include wisdom, clarity, oneness, unity and interconnectedness with all life. It is our source of life and the activation point of Reiki energy. The corresponding colours are purple, gold or white.

Balancing the Chakras with Reiki

The Chakras or energy centres of the body are major storehouses of information which relate to our physical, psychological, emotional and psycho-spiritual selves. In relation to healing, the Chakras give us a clear map of the overall health of a person on an energy level.

During a treatment we may need to balance a Chakra or a series of Chakras. By applying Reiki energy to each individual Chakra, we greatly assist in creating balance throughout the entire energy body.

Procedure:
1. Position yourself at the crown of the client.
2. Place palm over palm, doubling the hand Chakras over this energy centre and leave the hands at the Chakra point for approximately 5 to 10 minutes. To enhance your treatment, you can also imagine the corresponding colours of each Chakra point.
3. Now, repeat the whole process for each of the following Chakra centres: Brow (indigo), Throat (blue), Heart (green), Solar Plexus (yellow), Sacral (orange) and Base (red).

During a treatment, it may be that only a few points require balancing however, as a sequence, this procedure aligns the individual and deeply touches the core of each centre of our being. Therefore I suggest we balance each centre from the crown to the base.

This is a very powerful technique for balancing the Chakras. It can be used instead of a full treatment, or for self-healing.

To finish the treatment, ground your client by gently massaging both feet and allow them some time to come around.

Group Reiki Treatment

Having an opportunity to receive a Reiki treatment from a group of Reiki practitioners is a wonderful thing where instead of receiving Reiki from one stream of energy, we receive many streams of energy. Similar to filling a bath tub with water, the body is a container. If we were to use not just one tap but several, the time it would take to fill the tub would be dramatically lessened. In this way, receiving a Reiki treatment from several people at once requires less treatment time. However, this should not limit the time we afford our client as one cannot over energise another with Reiki and it is always safe.

When working as a practitioner in a group setting with others, it is not really practical to try and cover all of the energy areas of the body, as you will generally get in the way of your fellow practitioners. Therefore, it is best to simply treat a few positions and leave the others to your Reiki comrades. In this way, you will give your client the best opportunity to receive comfortably, as much Reiki as they need.

Group treatments are often a powerful experience. Whether you are giving Reiki or are on the receiving end, the amount of energy is great and is a most wonderful experience for both practitioners and client.

Eastern Style Japanese Reiki Techniques

The following techniques come from the Japanese style of Reiki and are common techniques practiced in the Reiki Gakkai which is Mikao Usui's original Reiki learning society. This society is still practicing an unbroken tradition of Reiki, as originally taught by Usui, to this day.

Special acknowledgment to: Horoshi Doi who is a Member of the Reiki Gakkai. Horoshi Doi brought many of these methods to Canada in 1999 where some 60 Reiki Masters learnt the traditional Japanese Reiki practices for the very first time.

Byosen Reikan ho

Byosen Reikan-ho – The method for sensing imbalances with your hands

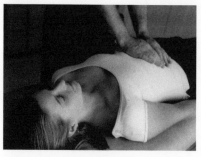

The words 'Byosen Reikan' describe the energy of a disease. It can be detected with your hands and will vary depending on the severity and condition of the disease from person to person. Byosen Reikan literally means: 'energy sensation of sickness' (imbalance/disease). Byo means: 'disease, sickness' and Sen means: 'before, ahead, previous, future, precedence'. Rei means: 'energy, soul, spirit' and Kan means: 'emotion, feeling, sensation'. Ho means: 'technique, method or way'. This is an original technique from Mikao Usui which can be facilitated for yourself or others.

When detecting a Byosen you will feel sensations such as tingling, tickling, pulsating, or piercing, pain, numbness, heat, cold and so forth; these sensations are called 'Hibiki'. You may even feel an ache in your hands or even up your arms in more serious cases. Whenever disease is present there will be a Byosen, even when the client is unaware of a physical condition. If you sense a Byosen in someone's body and work on it until it disappears, the related disease (or potential disease) will either completely heal or never manifest on the physical level.

It is important to note that the Byosen may show up in an obvious place (like over or near the diseased part), or somewhere that seems completely unrelated.

The ability to sense a Byosen will vary greatly from person to person. Some practitioners will readily detect it whilst others will need to take time to develop this ability.

The Technique:

1. Sit or stand comfortably next to the recipient.
2. Place your hands in the Gassho Mudra*, calm your mind and say silently *"I will begin Byosen Reikan-ho now"*.
3. Place your hands on or slightly above the body, move them slowly around and sense what you feel. You are looking for areas where

---

* Gassho Mudra: The Mudra of the hands in prayer position at heart level.

you feel something different from the overall general sensation (i.e. heat, cold, tingling, or an absence of sensation).

4. When you sense a 'Hibiki', hold your hands over the area. The Hibiki will increase and then decrease; this is one cycle, which will repeat as long as your hands are over the body. Now place your hands on the body where you sense the Byosen. The longer you hold your hands on a spot, the more cycles you will feel. With each cycle, the peak of the Hibiki diminishes slightly. Keep your hands on the area for a minimum of one cycle.

The Gassho Mudra

5. Move your hands to the next Byosen and repeat step 4.
6. When you have completed the entire body, place your hands in the Gassho Mudra and give thanks.

Reiji ho

Reiji-ho – The method of allowing Reiki to guide you

Once a student is confident working with detecting Byosen, then Reiji-ho is taught. This is a technique for allowing the Reiki energy to guide you. Your hands are drawn to places on the client's body, wherever Reiki energy is required. By doing Reiji-ho, you will become more aware of the subtle energy of the body.

With on-going practice, your intuition will heighten and you will be more able to develop greater trust in what you are sensing during a Reiki treatment.

A literal translation of 'Reiji' is: 'sign from spirit (energy)'. Rei means: 'energy, spirit, universal, or soul' and Ji means: 'show, indicate, point out, express, display'. Ho means: 'technique, method or way'. This is an original technique from Mikao Usui, which can be applied to yourself and others.

The Technique:

1. Sit or stand comfortably next to the recipient.
2. Place your hands in the Gassho Mudra, calm your mind and focus your attention on the Tanden*. After a moment, say silently *"I will begin Reiji-ho now"*.
3. Feel your body completely relaxing, releasing all tensions. Call upon the Reiki energy, asking that you and/or your client be completely filled with Reiki energy. Now imagine that your client and yourself are enveloped in this healing energy. When you feel ready, move to step 4.
4. Move your hands *(still in Gassho)* up to your third eye *(forehead)* and ask the Reiki energy to guide your hands to those places in need of energy. Your hands will be guided or drawn like a magnet to areas of imbalance in the recipient's body. When each part is sufficiently balanced, your hands will be guided to the next spot. This process continues until all imbalanced places in the body have been energised. The Reiki energy will guide you to where the recipient requires energy, for however long is necessary.
5. If you feel you are not flowing with this experience or you do not feel where you need to go next, you may place your hands back to your third eye between each hand placement and request guidance for the next position.
6. When the healing is complete, your hands will feel like they wish to return to the Gassho Mudra. This completes the treatment.

Meditating with the hands in Dhyani Mudra concentrating awareness on the Tanden.

---

*The Tanden is situated at the navel and represents a store house of Reiki energy.

Tanden Chiryo ho

Tanden Chiryo-ho – The method of de-poisoning the body

 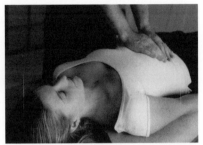

This technique will assist the body in removing poisons and toxins. Toxins can be physical, mental, or emotional. This process can be done on yourself or others. Tanden means: 'energy vessel', Chiryo means: 'medical treatment' and Ho means: 'treatment, method or way'. This is an original technique from Mikao Usui.

The Technique:
1. Sit or stand comfortably next to the recipient.
2. Place your hands in the Gassho Mudra, calm the mind and say silently *"I will begin Tanden Chiryo-ho now"*.
3. Place one hand on the Tanden (1 to 1 ½ inches below the navel) and the other hand on the forehead (third-eye area). Sense the energy in the hand on the forehead and generate the strong wish for the Reiki energy to remove all poisons from the body. Say this silently in your mind. Hold this position for 5 minutes. (Imagine that during this time, all the toxins of the body are been stirred up).
4. Remove your hand from directly touching the client's forehead and move your hand down just above the body, moving slowly towards the Tanden, until both hands are at the Tanden, side by side. Take some time to slowly move your hand from above the recipient's forehead, down to the Tanden. As you move your hand slowly (above the body), imagine that your hand is drawing all of the bodies toxins, just as a net would catch fish in the sea. Imagine all of these toxins being drawn towards the Tanden area.
5. Now, with both hands side by side at the Tanden, you can imagine all the toxins are being dissolved by the Reiki energy and the whole

body is being filled with healing energy.

6. One can imagine these toxins leaving the body, like smoke rising from a fire above your hands and dissolving in space. Do this for 10 to 15 minutes.

7. When complete, return your hands in the Gassho Mudra and give thanks.

Gyoshi ho

Gyoshi-ho – The method for healing with the eyes

This technique is used for sending healing energy with the eyes. Gyoshi means: 'gaze, stare or fixation' and Ho means: 'technique, method or way'. In the Usui Hikkei (Usui practitioner manual), it states that Reiki emanates from all body parts, but is strongest from the hands, eyes and the breath.

Gazing with your eyes defocussed is a soft and gentle way to direct the Reiki energy. Combined with a feeling of love and compassion, this method is very beneficial. One looks without staring, at the place requiring healing energy and senses the Reiki transferring from the eyes to the recipient.

Imagine this transference of healing energy like beams of soft light from your eyes to the recipient.

This is an original technique from Mikao Usui.

The Technique:

This technique can be done during a regular Reiki treatment, or any-time you wish to send Reiki to a person, place, object etc… It is impor-tant not to stare or look aggressively while doing Gyoshi simply gaze at the area with your eyes slightly defocussed. This technique can be done with or without the traditional Reiki symbols.

1. Gaze at the place you wish to send Reiki, with your eyes slightly defocussed. Feel loving Reiki energy pouring out through your eyes and going into the recipient. You can imagine this as a stream of blue light, or incorporate other colours where appropriate. See the recipient as being whole and perfect as they are. One should not

bring any judgement towards the person.

2. Visualize the symbols of your choice going out of your eyes, embedding in the area of your gaze. Know that the symbol will go to the cause of the condition, and heal it in the most appropriate way. Simply be with the person and the Reiki energy.

3. Continue until you feel you are guided to move to the next position or until you feel it is complete.

4. Complete your treatment with your hands returning to the Gassho Mudra and give thanks.

NOTE: This technique can be incorporated into hands-on healing or any other Shoden or Okuden techniques.

Koki-ho

Koki-ho – The method for healing with the breath

This technique is used for sending healing energy with your breath. Koki means: 'exhalation, breath or breathing' and Ho: means 'technique, method or way'.

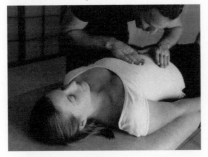

When you feel heat in your mouth, nose or chest you can send Reiki with your breath. A particularly helpful technique when you are working with clients who have been burnt, or whom you cannot otherwise touch. This technique is also of benefit in directing energy into the body or energy centres.

For Second Degree students, the Reiki symbols can also be directed using this method.

This is an original technique from Mikao Usui.

The Technique:

Do this technique during a regular Reiki treatment, in absent healing, or anytime you wish to send Reiki to a person, place, object, situation etc...

1. Breathe in Reiki energy through your nose and crown and imagine this forms a sphere of healing energy and light in your Tanden.

2. Breathe gently out through your mouth *(lips in an 'O' shape)* to the area you wish to send Reiki. Imagine the sphere of healing energy is

entering into the area we are blowing and completely filling it with healing energy.

3. If we are using the Reiki symbols, imagine the symbol forming in your mouth on the in breath and being infused when directed to the person, place, or object etc…

Heso Chiryo ho

Heso Chiryo-ho – The method of navel healing

This technique addresses an important area to heal disease – the navel.

 The navel is considered by some to be the centre of the body and is our (umbilical) connection to the Divine. Healing in this way can assist with healing the pain of separation from the source of life and to gain a sense of unity with Divine energy. It is also very useful in healing a range of illnesses. One can also utilise this method to heal issues of separation from our birth Mother. When separation occurs at birth, this trauma is stored in our psyche and energetically creates a wound in this area. By applying concentrated Reiki into this point, the Reiki energy assists with healing these issues of the feminine principle and healing separation from all things.

Heso means: 'navel', Chiryo means: 'medical treatment' and Ho means: 'treatment, method or way'. This is an original technique from Mikao Usui, which can be applied to oneself or another.

The Technique:

1. Sit or stand comfortably next to the recipient.
2. Place your hands in the Gassho Mudra, calm your mind and say silently *"I will begin Heso Chiryo-ho now"*.
3. Place one hand on the Tanden, with the middle finger inserted into the navel (or just above it) and the other hand on the back, opposite the navel (slide one hand under the recipient's back). On yourself, place your other hand on top the hand touching the navel and use the law of correspondence to state that your top hand now corresponds to the hand position on your back, opposite the navel. This option may also be used if placing the hand under the client

proves too difficult. Once in position, sense the pulse *(felt in the tip of your middle finger)* aligning with the Universal energy flow.

4. Imagine, during the procedure, that healing energy is flowing into this point, clearing all trauma and creating balance and wholeness.
5. Hold this position until you feel the healing is complete. Approximately 10 to 20 minutes.
6. When complete, return your hands into the Gassho Mudra and give thanks.

The Japanese Reiki techniques as discussed previously represent just some of the methods which were taught by Mikao Usui and are continued today as part of the traditional Japanese Reiki teachings.

4
The Practice of Reiki

When to Consider a Reiki Practice
Establishing a Reiki practice is something which evolves out of on-going Reiki treatments. For the dedicated practitioner, there comes a time when one is ready to move from giving Reiki treatments at the student level to charging for services as a qualified practitioner.

It goes without saying that one should attain a certain degree of experience and training prior to taking this step. For practitioners who wish to establish a Reiki practice, it is recommended to wait until they have completed the Second Degree of Reiki (*jap*: Okuden) before offering one's services to the general public.

In order to give treatments in a suitable manner, one requires a treatment room in which to practice. It is necessary to create a space for healing in order to convey a professional approach and one that will support healing for others.

The Treatment Room
Although a treatment room is not a requirement to give Reiki, *(as all that is necessary is placing your hands on the body)* a space dedicated to practice can greatly increase the meditative qualities and relaxation of a treatment, thereby enhancing a serene setting for Reiki.

If you choose to set up a treatment room, here are some guidelines which you may find useful:

- Select a room away from high traffic areas.
- Create a safe, relaxing, quiet space. Use soft colours, with light blinds over windows. Plants can help create a natural atmosphere.
- Dim the lights or light candles to help create ambience.

In term of practitioner equipment, you will need:

- a massage table.
- a comfortable rolling chair *(preferably height adjustable)*.
- pillows *(for the head and under the knees)*.
- a box of tissues and a blanket.
- a CD player, and a collection of soft soothing music, *(be sure to have music which your client finds relaxing)*.
- Aromatherapy diffuser and oils, add pleasant aromas and aid in relaxation or high quality Japanese incense. Be sure to find out if your client has any allergies to incense and never use too much. Always avoid using cheap oils or incense.

Practitioner Equipment in Detail

When it comes to adding professionalism as well as comfort to your Reiki practice, it is necessary to purchase some quality Reiki equipment. The most essential item is your Reiki treatment table. This is perhaps the most important piece of equipment you will ever buy for Reiki and one should therefore not skimp on purchasing a sound treatment table. Although one need not go to extreme lengths in purchasing the top of the range treatment table with hydraulic height adjustment, the Reiki table should have some practical options for a professional practice. Your table should ideally feature a face hole for when your client needs to receive a localized Reiki treatment on their back, in which case a preferred option is to have an adjustable head cradle.

You might also consider a height adjustable stool which will enable easy access to your client when lying down or even a height adjustable table. Having a height adjustable table is an option which is not often used, as many practitioners will have a table made to order specifying their height when standing. The correct height of your treatment table will ensure you will be at a comfortable position when giving treatments for extended periods of time. Because Reiki treatments involve laying the hands on the body for several minutes in one position, many practitioners opt for a height adjustable stool as this is easier on the legs and especially the arms as you can use the table to lean your elbows on when giving treatments seated.

It is also worth mentioning that when giving treatments one should position the treatment table in the room so it is possible to move completely around it, enabling you full access to every treatment position without disturbing your client.

Music

Another important part of the Reiki treatment experience is the accompanied ambient music. It is important to choose music that is fairly level throughout. The last thing you need is a CD which is full of sudden surprises like increased tempo or rapid drumming for example.

Reiki music which does not have lyrics is best as you may find that both you and your client focusses on the words, which can prevent deeper states of consciousness being reached. Having said this, CDs with mantras or chanting can be of benefit as their repetitive nature will take both the giver and receiver into a deep and peaceful state of mind. Remember to ask your client which types of music they like or encourage them to bring a copy of their own favourite music or play their favourite CD from your collection when giving on-going treatments.

Other tools of the trade

Other equipment may also include an aromatherapy vaporiser or incense. If you are going to use aromatherapy oils with a vaporiser, or incense for that matter, it's recommended that you first determine whether your client has any allergies to these and if in doubt, do not use them. When using aromatherapy oils, one should be well informed of the properties of these oils and which ones are suitable for relaxation and calming. One should also be aware of how much to use. Aromatherapy can have a very powerful effect and in some cases can be harmful, so an educated approach is best.

Where to Practice
Your Home

For Practitioners on a budget, starting a practice from home has its advantages as one will not incur extra rental costs to hire a room. Your home is generally more comfortable and familiar to you and you need not travel in order to give a treatment. Other benefits include:

- Greater flexibility in appointment times, as you can fit them into your schedule.
- You don't have any long term contract agreements as is the case when hiring a room in a healing centre or office.

Although there are benefits, practising from home has its downfalls. These include:

- The potential disruptions from family, friends dropping in or pets disrupting your session.
- Your clients may question your professionalism as you may not be able to offer a waiting room as well as the problem of having to constantly arrange a room in your home which may not be exclusively used for your treatments.
- There are the potential problems from your local council, who may not allow you to run a business from home as well as parking issues.
- Noisy or disgruntled neighbours.

Renting a Room

When considering the option of renting a room, whether this is from a complementary therapy centre or office, there are again pros and cons.
   Some of the advantages in renting a room include:

- You won't have the problem of potential interruptions from family members and you may have the option of having a receptionist who can take bookings *(this adds tremendous credibility).*
- In most cases clients will have a waiting room if they are early; and you can often network your client base with other therapists in the same building.
- Many centres also have the option of credit card facilities for easy payments by your clients.
- You can also share the rent of your room, as well as having your space set up for the sole purpose of treating others.

Of course there are some disadvantages as well. These include:

- The costs and commitments to paying for a room to practice from. You may not get a constant flow of clients and therefore will need to pay the rent regardless of whether it is busy or quiet.
- You may not have as much freedom to see your clients as the room may only be available at certain times as well as having to travel to and from your practice.
- There is the potential problem of your practice being located on a busy street or highway thus adding to the problem of noise.
- Potential for noisy neighbours.

Some other things to consider when choosing premises to practice from include:

- Client accessibility – is the location central to bus and train lines?
- Does your room have access to wheelchair and disability ramps and toilets?
- What is the parking like and is it close to your centre?
- Are there time limits for parking which may be expensive and might otherwise influence clients booking with you?

You will also need to determine when most people will be able to see you for treatments and whether you will only offer treatments during office hours or also during the evenings or on weekends. You will also need to determine whether your treatment room will be available during these preferred times.

The other thing to consider is the overall appearance of your treatment room. You can add much credibility to your practice if you make the room a sanctuary for relaxation and peace. You can do much to add peaceful ambience to your room use your creativity and ask others for feedback. A fresh pair of eyes and some honest feedback on your treatment room can be very rewarding.

Reiki on the move – becoming a Mobile Therapist
Another way to practice is to become a mobile Reiki therapist. Mobile Reiki therapists can actually tap new clientele which may include:

- The elderly.
- Mothers with small children.
- People with disabilities.
- People who lack transport.
- People who have phobias such as the fear of open spaces (agoraphobia) or fears of public transport, such as riding on trains.

There are advantages to being a mobile Reiki therapists:
These include:

- No rental costs for hiring a room or contract.
- You will reach more people.
- Your clients will feel more comfortable being treated in the comfort of their own home or office.

Some of the disadvantages may include:

- You may not have all the facilities you require to accommodate your treatment.
- You will have additional travel costs and time travelling to and from your client's home or office.
- You will be giving your treatment in an unfamiliar setting with no real idea of what arrangement you will encounter upon arrival.
- You will need to transport your treatment table and other equipment.
- You also might encounter the annoyance of turning up to give your mobile session only to find your client is not at home or has forgotten about your appointment.

A way to counter this is to arrange payment prior to giving the treatment. This not only secures your costs, it is a sure way of guaranteeing your client will be there when you show up.

In order to counter some of these potential problems you might encourage a regular client to purchase their own treatment table. You will also need to factor in your travel time, therefore a higher fee should be charged for making house or office calls.

Working as an on-site Therapist

If you are fortunate enough to be offered a position as an on-site Reiki Practitioner, there are numerous benefits which include inheriting an already established client base. This means you will have no marketing or advertising costs. The company will promote you, thus ensuring on-going work as well as the inevitable referrals which will come via 'word of mouth'. This can also translate into obtaining further private treatments outside your on-site practice. Examples of on-site Therapist settings include: Staff treatments in large offices, Mining sites, and corporate events to name a few.

5
Reiki and Money

Re-defining our view of money

In the area of healing a common issue is placing a set value on Reiki. This comes from the way many of us had the words drummed into our heads: *"You cannot be spiritual and wealthy"*. For many, the spiritual martyr inside us regularly affirms that we are not being spiritual if we charge money for giving Reiki.

I often hear from Reiki therapists that they do not charge for giving Reiki because *"it's not spiritual"*. If a Reiki therapist chooses not to charge for their time then this is fine provided they have an alternative source of income. Some people prefer to have Reiki as a hobby and do so because they feel uncomfortable charging for their services, but let us take a look for a moment at the truth of Spiritual marketing.

Over the years I have heard from many people in the Reiki field as well as many other spiritual and new age arts that they do not consider it spiritual to earn from their spiritual practice, let alone make a lot of money from their practice. They feel that by receiving money for giving Reiki is directly violating spiritual laws.

What many fail to see is that abundance is our birthright and being abundant is spiritual. One need only look at nature to see her wealth. The fact of the matter is that whether someone delivers the post or administers healing, both offer a benefit to others. The truth of the matter is that all work is spiritual work.

When we look at what holds people back from being financially successful in their Reiki practice, we find the biggest thing standing in the way are self-limiting beliefs. It is a well known spiritual law that *'as we think, so we become'* which also applies to our self-worth with regard to abundance and prosperity.

You must think as you would become. If you are to succeed in your

Reiki practice, not only spiritually but financially, then you need to alter your mindset from one of lack, to one of prosperity.

If you are genuinely interested in furthering your spiritual knowledge about Spiritual Prosperity then I highly recommend the following books:

- *Rich Dad, Poor Dad* – by Robert Kiyosaki, plus others in his series.
- *Think and Grow Rich* – by Napoleon Hill.
- *The Dynamic Laws of Prosperity* – by Catherine Ponder.

How to earn a living and still be spiritual

You can get started on becoming successful by looking at your motivation.

The simple logic is to ask yourself: *'Why do I wish to begin a Reiki Practice?'*

When we ask ourselves this question some of our answers might include:

'To help others who are in need'
'To grow in myself by healing others'
'To be a spiritual example to others'
'To improve my Reiki abilities by working with other people' etc…

You might wish to include your own ideas by writing your personal reasons below:

_____
_____
_____

Now look at your answers, and ask yourself the question, how can I offer my services to others if no one knows I exist?

The answer is, you can't. Promoting yourself is inevitable if you are going to benefit others. In order to continue offering your service, your services need to be reciprocal. It is important to closely examine the benefit of exchange. When you offer a service to another, you set in motion a benefit to that persons' life, they will be more able to benefit others.

The fact that you have helped them means that they in accordance with the laws of Karma, (cause and effect) owe you something in return. When we charge for our services we create an opportunity for the recipient to return our gift and thus create a karmic balance. Not to offer a means for exchange is to actually create a karmic debt. When you think about it, you help the person on one hand but hinder them on the other if you don't offer a means of exchange for your service.

It is actually your responsibility to charge for your services, thereby creating perfect balance and an equal exchange for services rendered.

How much to charge

Many new Reiki Practitioners who take the step of charging for their services often have some difficulty determining a fair value for their Reiki Treatments. Many sell themselves short by thinking that they are but a channel for Universal energy and are not even doing the healing, Reiki is. In part, this is true but healing does not happen all by itself. The Reiki channel must be there to facilitate the transference of Reiki to another.

Reiki needs you just as much as you need Reiki. If you are not there to facilitate the treatment, be this in person or via the distant healing procedure, no healing will occur.

We need to look at the fact that we are not charging for the Reiki energy, we are charging for our time. The price we charge should also be indicative of our level of expertise, experience, and training.

One way to determine what you may wish to charge for your time is to call on others who are practicing Reiki and ask them what they charge. By doing this you will also get an idea of what the accepted fee structure is for your location. As a general guide many Reiki practitioners charge a fee similar to that of a regular massage treatment.

It is also important to set the right fee. Setting a fee that is too low can actually backfire and people can undervalue your service and Reiki's benefit. They may also think that you do not have enough experience or lack credible training.

Setting a fee that is too high on the other hand, will leave potential clients being unable to afford your service. Therefore, you must strike a suitable balance so that your clients will value your service and be able to afford it on a regular basis.

Once you have established your treatment fee, you may need to review this from time to time to take into account increased costs, such as room rental and inflation. It is quite normal for most businesses to increase their prices every second year, so the same should apply to you.

Practitioner expenses

When you are determining your fee structure you also need to factor in your expenses. These might include: Government taxes, Rent for your room hire, travel time, maintaining your practitioner equipment, washing table covers, as well as public and professional liability insurance.

Creating Value

You can create a value of your healing work by establishing how unique your service is. In marketing this is called your 'U.S.P.', which stands for – "Unique Selling Proposition".

What is it that makes what you do different from anyone else?

Make a list now of what you offer, as well as all the benefits that one might gain from receiving your service.

_____

_____

_____

_____

Out of your list what makes your service unique? You need to determine your U.S.P. and then let your clients know about it. Even if your service seems like everyone else's, you can create a perceived value. For example, you could make your U.S.P. the way you give a treatment that is unique, or that you offer a comprehensive treatment. Finding your U.S.P. is a personal journey because no one else can find it for you.

Concessions

Some practitioners like to offer concessions for seniors, students or the unemployed. This ultimately is your choice. An alternative to offering discounts is to create special offers. Discounts mean that at the end of the day you will get less money for your time. Special offers, on the other hand can actually increase your hourly rate by creating additional business because they entice your clients to buy again. When we add a value or incentive to what we offer, we actually create more business.

Some offers might include a VIP earnings card, where your 3rd treatment is free. Other incentives may include a 10% discount when three treatments are paid in full in advance. Either way, special offers like this, mean more treatments, which equals on-going business for you.

Often some of the best forms of advertising are by word of mouth. You might reward your ongoing clients with a free treatment when they successfully refer five of their friends to you.

Rules of Practice – Cancellations and Confirmations

Now that we have determined our financial worth, we need to determine the rules for payment. It is inevitable that at some time during your practice, your client will cancel an appointment and in some cases, just not show. You need to determine whether you will charge a cancellation fee.

Many practitioners require 24 hours cancellation notice. In the event your client calls more than 12 hours prior to their appointment some may opt for a 50% cancellation fee, whilst other practitioners take the risk in their stride.

One way to counter this problem is to secure payment prior to the appointment. Credit card bookings over the phone are a great way to do this. You can be sure that if your client has paid in advance, they will move mountains to get there and even if they don't, your time is paid for all the same.

Some Reiki practitioners may argue that they would never consider charging a cancellation fee, thinking that they will lose their client, however you need to consider your time and the preparation it takes to give a treatment. Consider these points:

- You should be compensated when you have arranged your day around your clients booking.
- You should be compensated for the time it takes to set up your treatment room.
- You should be compensated for the mental preparation to give the treatment.
- You should be compensated for lost appointments, when another client might otherwise have booked that session time.

These are questions you need to ask yourself and then determine whether this is an option you wish to consider. If you do, you will need to effectively communicate your cancellation policy over the phone when the booking is made, as well as having your payment terms and conditions clearly displayed in your treatment room or office, thus reducing any potential misunderstandings.

Another way to avoid missed treatments where your client simply forgets or cancels is to phone a day or half day prior, to confirm the appointment. For the cost of a local phone call, you can save yourself time and money.

Getting Paid and Payment Options

It is often at the end of giving a treatment that most practitioners settle the account. However you may wish to do this when your client arrives for the following reasons:

After receiving a Reiki treatment, your client may be in a vulnerable or in a highly peaceful and relaxed state. In most cases so will you. It has been my experience that on a number of occasions both my client and I completely forgot the payment, not realizing until they were long gone.

It also may be the case that you do not wish the person to have to deal with money after the treatment so that they can simply leave to enjoy the serene space.

For many of us, money can make us tense, so sorting this out prior to the treatment, or well in advance, is highly recommended.

It is becoming more common to use credit card facilities to make payments and it seems this will only increase in the future. Therefore, it makes good business sense to have these facilities at your disposal. If you have many clients, electronic facilities are more costly, but save time and present a more professional presentation. However, for medium to small clientele base, manual facilities *(the old click-clack machine)* work just fine.

Provided you have some financial history most banks will approve the use of Merchant facilities *(Credit Cards)* in your business. With credit card facilities you will be able to receive payments for treatments over the phone, as well as mail order payments for advanced bookings.

The other thing to consider is that cash payments are becoming more rare these days. Another dinosaur is the old cheque book. If you are receiving cheques, be sure that your client's address is on the back of the cheque and add their phone number in case where the cheque "bounces". You will be glad you did so, as you will have a record and a way of making contact with them, ensuring you actually get paid.

Although this is an often uncomfortable subject for many, it is important to form clear boundaries with money from the start, which will enable you to avoid many of these potential problems.

6

Handling Enquiries

Making the most of the Telephone

Although email is fast becoming a leading means of communication, most people still prefer the personal touch that comes from speaking over the phone. The humble telephone is your most important piece of communication equipment, so it is wise to make the most of it. The following are some guidelines:

Obtaining a memorable number

Obtaining a phone number with similar or repeat digits is far more memorable to your clients. If you are looking at upgrading to a new number or require a new number for your Reiki practice, be sure to contact your phone company to see what's possible. In many cases a special request for repeat numbers will incur a higher fee, but it will be well worth it. Phone numbers with repeat numbers or with a rhythm will be more frequently recalled by your current and future clients.

For example, the number (08) 8855 8855 is far easier to recall than (08) 8435 2956. If you have the option of purchasing an existing number, consider the previous business which owned it. It can be a major problem to receive calls for something other than your business day in and day out.

It is also advisable to avoid phone numbers that have other connotations. There may be reasons why the phone number ending with 666 or 6969 are so readily available for use.

1800 and 1300 numbers

Free call numbers such as 1800 numbers are another option which you might consider. With a toll free number, your clients bear no expense in calling you, which can be an added incentive. However, unless you have a large turnover in clients and wish to support this constant flow, then you may not be able to justify the monthly fees as well as paying for your clients' calls. Other problems can be when your friends and family get wind of the fact that you have a free call number. They might start using your friendly service at your expense. With 1300 numbers, the caller only pays for a local call so 1300's suit interstate callers, which may not suit your business if you only treat people locally.

When the phone is running hot

When your phone is running hot, (*perhaps from implementing some of the suggestions in this book*), you might consider a messaging service, so missed calls can be taken by a telephone bureau. This way your prospective clients can speak to someone who will take their message. Nothing beats the human touch that comes from speaking to a person rather than a recorded message or answering machine.

On the flip side, every business will experience dry spells from time to time where no matter the amount of advertising the phone simply does not ring. The good news is that this presents an opportunity to improve your business and to review your current methods of promotion and advertising. When you are not busy treating clients, get busy promoting and improving your business. One should also consider promotions targeting your existing clientele.

I'll get back to you!

Let's face it, we all prefer to talk to the person we are calling and when we hear the words on an answering machine, *"Your call is important to us"* we can't help but think that if it really was that important, they might be there to answer the phone. Unless you have the option of a secretary for those working from an established premises, there are a few options for clients to leave a message:

Answering Machines

If you are in business and do not have a way for your clients to leave a message, then it is likely that you will not be in business for very long. Nothing is as frustrating as having no option to leave a message when you call a business.

In the case where you have an answering machine, then careful consideration should be made to your message. If you are not available to be there to answer the phone, then your answering machine message will be your new clients' first impression.

Therefore your message should sound positive, lively and friendly.

Here is an example which you might find useful:

> "Hello, you've reached (state your name) from (state your business name). I am either taking another call right now or giving a treatment, however I'm not far away and will get back to you as soon as I can. Please leave your name and phone number, slowly and clearly after the tone. Thanks for your call and have a great day! BEEP!"

What is your current answering machine message and have you thought about how you can make it more memorable or engaging? Take a few minutes now to re-write your message.

_____

_____

_____

_____

Once you have recorded your message, call yourself from another phone and listen to yourself. Do you sound like someone you would like to receive a Reiki treatment from? Ask some friends to call your number and listen to your message. Ask for constructive feedback then fine tune your message until it feels and sounds right.

Getting your message to sound right with variation in your voice is also important. You don't want to sound like you are reading a shopping list when you record your message so remember to make it lively and interesting. You might even wish to write your message greeting down and record it several times until it sounds just right.

Message Bank

Another option is to obtain a message bank service from your telephone carrier. This means that when you are talking to someone else, the person calling can leave a message on your message bank. This way you will not miss any calls. Again, make your message positive, lively and friendly. If your client encounters an engaged signal, they will more then likely not bother to call you again or will seek out another therapist, so message bank is a must for business.

Call waiting

Call waiting is another less attractive option which you may consider but I do not recommend it. This is when you are talking to a potential client and an annoying *BEEP, BEEP!* can be heard interrupting your conversation. When you hear the *BEEP, BEEP*, you could say: *"can I just put you on hold whilst I see who that is?"* meanwhile they are put on hold, having to listen to elevator music.

Please do not do this to your clients. When you say: *"can I just put you on hold whilst I see who that is"*, it says to your client that this other person who is interrupting your call is far more important than them.

Keep it personal and friendly and you will earn your clients respect and patronage.

Internet and Email

Many people are today making bookings via email. If you advertise your email address be sure to create one which reflects your business. Some example might be:

reikiheals@serviceprovider.com
feelbetternow@serviceprovider.com
healing4you@serviceprovider.com

These email addresses communicate the benefits of your service. Every time a client emails you, they are getting a positive re-enforcement that you can benefit them.

If you advertise email as a point of contact be sure to check your email regularly and by this I mean at least once a day. If someone emails you they want to hear from you as soon as possible. Email is not that different from a phone call. So if you can get back to your emails with speed and efficiency, your clients will feel they are important and respected. It's their time and money after all.

When you receive a reply, *(if you have set this out correctly, you will)*, then your future email correspondence should include an email signature.

An email signature means at the end of each email you send, an automatic signature of your contact details, as well as your '7 good reasons' to use your service or your U.S.P. are listed. You can even add your company logo to each email by following email programme software.

All this makes it easier for your clients to find your vital booking information. Business cards can be lost, but most people tend to keep emails in their inbox, for months, if not years.

If you do not have an email account, you can get email accounts online for free. Just visit: www.hotmail.com or www.yahoo.com, then click on the sign up email account button, follow the prompts and you'll be on your way. These setup guidelines are idiot proof so now even the village idiots have email.

For those who do not have an email account and are not internet savvy, then my advice is to get informed. In the last five years we have seen an enormous increase in the use of email. If you are not keen on computers take a short course on basic internet skills. In a matter of one hour, you'll be surfing the net and sending emails like a pro, or at least like a beginner. If you're not online, you're not in business.

7

Turning an enquiry into a booking

Answering Questions with confidence

Once you are over the hurdle of having clients call you, the next thing is to turn those enquiries into bookings. Some people will already be convinced they wish to use your service and will simply wish to book a time with you when they call.

Others will want to know several things and will ask many questions before making a commitment. The thing to remember is that if they are still asking questions, they are still interested. The following are some of the more frequently asked questions by people making enquiries. Below each question is a space where you can write your answers, have a go at this exercise now!

FAQ's

How can Reiki benefit my (insert an ailment) problem?

_____

_____

_____

_____

Does it work for everyone, and if so, how?

_____

_____

_____

_____

How long have you been doing Reiki?

_____

_____

_____

_____

Have you had any success with treating people with my (insert an ailment) condition?

_____

_____

_____

_____

How much do you charge for your treatments?

_____

_____

_____

_____

Do you offer any concessions?

_____

_____

_____

_____

When can I get a treatment?

_____

_____

_____

_____

Where are you located?

_____

_____

_____

_____

Where can I park?

_____

_____

_____

_____

How much is this going to cost me?

Of all the questions that arise out of an enquiry, the issue of 'how much' is one of the most motivating reasons for anyone taking the step to booking a treatment. When your future client asks you how much, don't blurt the price straight away. Instead tell them what they will get for their money first.

You might say for example, *"Can I explain to you what is involved with the treatment so you know what you are paying for?"* Then them the fee and add value to what you are offering. This is a great time to tell them about your special offer. For example: *"We also have a special offer, where if you pay in advance for three treatments, your third one is free, so you actually save $50".*

In this example your future client will now be thinking that they have saved $50.

Seven reasons to book with you

When communicating the benefits of your treatments you need to sell yourself.

It is said that if you can present seven good reasons why someone should part with their hard earned money, you will secure business.

In the following table you can list seven benefits from your treatments. You might include:

- Some of the health and relaxation benefits.
- Your professional service.
- Your sound experience and anything else which makes your service of benefit to your client.
  Remember your client is asking, *what's in it for me?*

You need to be able to communicate this. Listing these seven good reasons, can become part of all your promotional materials by including this list at the end of your emails, on letterheads, business cards, and press advertising. People want results and they want to know it is safe and that it can improve their health and wellbeing.

Stop reading now and get to work on creating your seven good reasons.

1. _____
2. _____
3. _____

4. _____

5. _____

6. _____

7. _____

8

Promotional Materials

Business Cards – Your Mobile Advertisement

Now that you have established your worth and why people should seek you out as a credible Reiki practitioner, you now need to provide your future clients with promotional materials in the form of business cards, a brochure, email information, free reports and creating a website. Perhaps the easiest and the most important is your business card.

Your business card is your miniature flyer. Your card represents you and your service, so spare no expense in utilizing the front and back of your card. Some people prefer to keep their card rather 'Zen' to simply offer their name and phone number but although you are short on space with the average business card being 90mm x 55mm, don't hesitate to use both sides because the more you tell, the more you sell.

To give you an example, a friend of mine created his business card for Iridology. He decided to put an enormous amount of information on his card with an in-depth description of the benefits in microscopic style (4 point). This is type in 4 point. To add to the novelty he also gave out with his cards a little magnifying glass so people could read the 500 words on the benefits of his services.

You'd be surprised just how many people took the time to read his card. Now I am not suggesting you do this, yet it is not necessary to make a business card look like a business card. If you can make your business card tell your reader why they should call you, then your business card has done its job. Be creative, flag down their interest and remember: 'The more you tell, the more you sell'.

Graphic Design

When it comes to producing your flyers and business cards, unless you have the skills in desktop publishing and have a background in graphic design I strongly suggest you employ the skills and creative talents of a graphic designer.

If you attempt to design and produce your own flyers, they will, in more cases than not, look home made and thus convey a non-professional message to your potential clients.

When selecting a graphic designer, it is not necessary to go direct to a big graphic design studio as the fees per hour can be higher than what you may charge and when you take into account the amount of time it can take to get your cards just right, you may find you have spent a great deal, even before going to press.

One way to get around this is to look for a freelance graphic designer. Often graphic designers who have just completed their training, will be looking for new jobs for their folio and will be happy to offer you a reduced rate just to add 'real jobs' to their folio *(I know because I used to be one!)*.

When arranging a quote for your design job, always arrange a written quote prior to commencing the project and get your graphic designer to sign on this agreed price. In this way, you can be sure that if you need to go overtime, you will not suffer financially as a result. If the graphic designer is worth their salt, they will know how to quote for a fair price, and this will often reflect a better quote from a big graphic design studio.

It is also advisable to get more than one quote for the same job as prices will vary from one designer to another. As part of selecting your graphic designer, you need to ensure they are of a suitable standard, so be sure to arrange a meeting to view their work or visit their website (if they have one) and check out their style and ability.

You may also wish to determine whether they have skills in website production because you can then translate the same design elements from your business card and flyer to a future website with little difficulty, as you would have already established branding for your stationery and promotional materials.

In-House Printing Designers

Some printers now offer in-house graphic design. Although they usually charge fewer fees per hour than graphic design studios, they can lack the creative flair of graphic designers. As with freelance, studio or in house designers, you will need to do your homework to determine which designer is most suitable in their technical and creative ability.

DIY Desktop Publishing

If you are looking to save money, then DIY Desktop Publishing may be an entry level option for creating your business cards and flyers. Many desktop publishing programmes now offer ready made templates for business cards and flyers, where you simply insert your details and the template will automatically change the type face, and colors to suit your needs.

Many of these software programmes offer diverse choices and herein lies a concern. You will have an option of choosing several different type faces and effects such as drop shadows, wacky fonts and clip art images for your flyers.

The principle motto is K.I.S.S. *(keep it simple sweetheart or stupid, as the case may be)*. A tendency is to put several type faces on the same card with every effect so as to make your card stand out. However, the result does stand out, but not in a nice way. You want to be remembered for how your card reflects your business, not how impressive and diverse your desktop publishing programme can be.

For more information on desktop publishing read the 'for Dummies' series. Such as: 'Desktop publishing for Dummies'

Another alternative is to take a short course in how to operate these publishing software programs. Many local schools offer after hours training, or you may wish to employ the private tuition of a graphic designer to teach you how to use them.

Getting ready for the printer

Once you have come up with a design that you are happy with, be this via the graphic designer, in-house designer, or relying on your DIY desktop publishing, you will need to save the document in a format that your printer will be able to use. Failing to do this will result in additional time and untold irritation for both you and the printer.

If you have a graphic designer doing your job then they will have already sorted this out for you. Most printers these days accept the format of PDF for printing. In most design programs such as WORD, COREL DRAW, QUARK and PAGEMAKER, you will have the option of saving your file as a High Resolution PDF. This file (providing it is not too big) can then be emailed to your printer, ready for production.

Email and Free Reports

You may be asking yourself, what is a free report? A free report is an email information page which gives your clients an overview of the product or service you are offering in 'lay mans' terms. Your free report should include a description of your service, a description of what Reiki is, the benefits of treatments, testimonials, a special offer to entice readers and a call to action. For example, a call to action might be: *"make a booking within 7 days of receiving this email and get a free gift valued at $20".*

When it comes to free reports, people want information but they do not want the hassle of phoning someone and this is where a free report *(which can be emailed or even posted in the mail)* comes in handy. In effect a free report is a mini website, and if you have a website the email free report is an excellent way to introduce your reader to your service with a 'click here' button to link it directly to your site if they want more information.

Testimonials
Testimonials speak volumes and if you can obtain these from people of standing, more the better. Therefore, don't ask your next of kin (like your mother for example) to write words of praise, unless your mother happens to be a medical doctor or professor of some repute.

Testimonials should only be a few lines or even one line, stating clearly how your client has benefitted from your treatments. One thing you might wish to do, is offer some free Reiki treatments in exchange for testimonials. If you already have some clients, ask them at the end of your treatment if they would mind writing a few words explaining what they got out of your session. Be sure to ask them if you have their permission to use their testimonials *(provided it's a positive response)* in your future advertising.

The best way to ask for a testimonial is by telling your client or friend that it is for use as a testimonial. Although you should encourage constructive criticism, a juicy testimonial is what you are after, so set the scene from the beginning. You will be surprised just how many people are willing to write you a complimentary report.

Testimonials can then be used on your business cards, website, brochures, flyers, email signatures and the like to tell the world just how amazing you truly are.

Gift Vouchers
Gift vouchers are another item which you should offer and regularly

advertise to your existing clientele. In my treatment room I have a large display and sign for gift vouchers. An example of how your gift voucher might read...

"This gift voucher entitles the bearer to a 1 hour Reiki treatment with (your name). Certified Reiki practitioner (of the Usui Reiki lineage, or school you studied with, or Reiki membership you have gained to add to your credibility)".

You will often find that by advertising your gift vouchers, especially before Christmas as a gift for the person who has everything, this can bring in new clientele.

It is advisable to put an expiry date on all your gift vouchers, otherwise, five years later, the recipient will call you saying, my friend *(of whom by this time, you have no recollection)* bought me this gift voucher. In the meantime, you may have moved your business or put up your prices. A reasonable time frame is one to three months to use the voucher.

9

Advertising: Where and How

Where to Advertise? – Local or National

The age old question of where to advertise depends on where you practice Reiki and how far you wish to travel, (if at all) to share your healing gifts with others. If you want people to come to your premises or home for your treatments, there is not much point in advertising to potential clients who live hours away. Unless you're the greatest healer on earth, they are not likely to travel vast distances to receive a treatment from you.

If you offer mobile treatments on the other hand, and are prepared to travel to give treatments to others, you first need to determine how far you are willing to travel. Once you have established your distance, it makes little sense to advertise in publications beyond this boundary.

Your local community newspaper or magazine can be a great resource and one should not underestimate the benefits of these mediums for advertising.

Knowing your target audience

The next thing you should consider is who your target audience is? There is not much use in advertising in *'Guns and Ammo'* magazine, just because they have a great advertising offer too good to refuse. You need to decide who are the people looking for your services. This is called establishing your target audience. On the other hand, if you advertise in very wide mediums, you may get lost in all the other services on offer. So it makes sense to research various magazine readerships and test these mediums before committing to a series of advertisements. Many advertising sales people will offer you great deals for advertising the same ad over six issues, but if your ad does not work for the first, it will not work for the other five.

Remember, you need to check the results of all your advertising. You can not afford not to.

Yellow Pages
How to stand out from the crowd

Reiki is usually listed under its own heading, or under the category of 'Alternative Health Therapies'. You would be surprised just how little you need to spend on yellow pages advertising to stand out from the crowd. For Reiki Therapists, I recommend advertising that asks your potential client to find out more.

Here is an example which entices your reader to find out more.

Your name and business name in bold – *Qualified Reiki Therapist.*

Need energy? Feel better now! Satisfaction Guaranteed. To find out how, phone: (your phone number) or visit: www.yourwebsite.com

In this example, bold heading your name and business name will draw the reader to your listing and you may even consider the bold heading in a Red Spot colour. This will draw the readers' eye even more so.

Let us now look at why this simple ad works. The statement: *"Need energy? Feel Better now!* identifies their potential problem and offers a solution to their problem. It also calls them to act with the statement: *'Feel better now!'*

The statement: *'Qualified Therapist'* tells your future client that you have credibility and know what you are doing. You are qualified and able to help them with their problems. With the statement: *'Satisfaction Guaranteed'* you are removing the element of risk by telling your potential client that they will feel satisfaction by receiving your treatment and that you are so sure of the effectiveness of your treatment you are willing to guarantee it.

The statement: *'To find out how, phone: (your phone number) or visit: www.yourwebsite.com'* gives your potential client the opportunity to find out more information via your website or by calling you.

If you do not have a website, you can offer a Free Report. In this case, your last line can read as follows: *'To find out how, email: yourname@ serviceprovider.com for a Free E-Information Pack or phone: (your phone number)'*

As you can see, every word counts and drives home a clear message. If you create your ad well, you will be successful in flagging down new clients.

Press Advertising

Press advertising is another powerful medium which need not cost the earth. Small space advertisements can really have a hypnotic effect on the reader. One of the best ways to have your ad read, is to not make your ad look like an ad.

The thing you should ask yourself is 'why do people buy a newspaper?' Do they buy it to read the advertising or do they read it for the articles?

You may have guessed that it is not for the advertising, so if advertising is the very thing your reader is not interested in, why not make your ad look like an article?

One way to achieve this is to produce an ad which looks like a newspaper article. This is where a strong headline does over 80% of the work for you.

Here are some proven attention grabbing headlines which have worked well in the past.

> *"10 Steps to renewed vitality"*
> *"The 'Hands-on' approach to healing revealed"*
> *"How the secret to health and healing is in the palm of your hand"*
> *"Natural Energy renewal technique revealed"*
> *"Astonishing facts about natural healing you must read"*
> *"You can heal yourself. Healing secrets revealed by local therapist"*
> *"Japanese hands on healing technique aids Cancer Patient"*
> *"Learn how a stress free life is in the palm of your hand"*
> *"Everyone's a healer!' Do you have what it takes?"*
> *"The truth about hands-on healing, the secrets revealed"*
> *"Healing secrets everyone should know"*
> *"10 steps to health and happiness with Reiki"*

Once you have flagged down your readers' interest, you can go on to reveal your important <u>must read</u> message.

The Power of Classified Ads

A classified advertisement is not a tool to revealing why someone should use your service, it is designed to elicit interest, so they are compelled to find out more. You don't have enough space to tell your story in a classified. You have only a few lines to secure interest and a call to action.

Just in the same way, the previous headlines offer powerful statements which grab readers interest and then follow with a story, the same headlines can be used in classified ads to similar effect.

Here are some examples:

> *Free report reveals: The 10 Steps to health and happiness with Reiki. Email: reiki@serviceprovider.com to find out how or call: (your phone number)*
>
> *Free Trial: Free Reiki Treatment from Qualified Therapist (Offer expires June 30th) Limited to the first 15 callers only. Ring Now! Ph: (your phone number)*
>
> *Reiki Healing for renewed vitality: Special offer: Buy one, Get one free! Don't miss your chance to experience Reiki today. Proven results from (your city's') leading therapist. Phone: (your phone number)*

Magazine Advertising

Magazine advertising, like press can be expensive, but unlike newspaper advertising where the readership is general, with magazines you can choose your target audience more specifically. There are many publications on the market these days on the subjects of health, spirituality, and personal growth. Just in the same way that it is not necessary to advertise a full page, small space advertising if done effectively can do wonders for your business.

Advertorial

Advertorial is a sure way to get your ad read, because it looks like an article and not an advertisement. It cannot be stressed enough that a good headline will flag down your reader. If we remember the motto, *'the more you tell, the more you sell'*, the better your chances are of securing business.

To illustrate this point, I once went to the trouble of calling the editor of a major holistic magazine in the UK, to ask which type face was used in their headlines, and body copy. In this case, I was advertising a series of Reiki seminars and as I wanted to make a big impression, I paid for a full page advertisement. I produced an advertisement which didn't resemble an ad at all. What I designed was an article which looked identical to the layout and design of the articles in the magazine. The editor of the magazine was a little nervous at my approach because no one had ever done this before. However, after reading the article (which was really an advertisement) she was happy with the content and granted approval. The result was that within one week we received more calls than we could handle and my class was fully booked in no time at all. Of course you need to offer something which is unique and of genuine interest to your readers. It is not enough to write an advertorial just for the sake of it.

When it comes to advertising, we are conditioned to do what everyone else is doing. If you are interested in obtaining new clients and reaching more people, you simply need to do the opposite of what everyone else is doing. When you do this, you stand out from the crowd, and readers take notice. When you are paying good money for advertising, the last thing you want is to have your ad resemble hundreds of other ads, which readers have become accustomed to ignoring.

Newsletters

Newsletters are one of the more affordable ways to advertise. Whether they are E-Newsletters (email) or hard copy newsletters, they can be another excellent way to reach specific audiences. One of the first things you need to consider is your target audience. The second is the number of newsletters circulated as well as the recipients' location. It is of little use advertising yourself for treatments in a newsletter whose subscribers are in another state or country. If you intend to go this way, you need to know that the recipients are local and that your readers have a potential interest in your service.

Radio Advertising

Radio is an all too often overlooked medium which can bring tremendous results. This is not necessarily in the form of the usual ads you get on commercial radio, because just like press and magazine advertising where ads looks like ads, so it is with radio. Most radio ads sound like radio ads and people tend to tune out or switch stations. People listen to the radio for music, the announcers, and interviews. Herein lies one of the best forms of radio advertising. You would be surprised just how many calls you will receive, by being interviewed on the radio about Reiki.

Call several radio stations *(not just the large commercial ones)* to see which stations have segments dedicated to Mind, Body, Spirit, or Health. Talk back radio segments are ideal and if you only have one minute air time or even a brief mention, it can still be enormously beneficial.

To give you an example, some years ago, one of our local and very well known radio celebrities attended our weekly Reiki clinic. He headed a popular morning talkback show and used some of his experiences as raw materials for his daily shows. Although the content had a 'tongue and cheek' feel the exposure was great. As a result the station received dozens of calls from people wanting to find out more about Reiki. Subsequently, our clinic (which was running at a modest pace), suddenly became booked out, two weeks in advance.

When Reiki receives a good endorsement from a high profile celebrity, albeit on the radio, the benefits are far reaching. Publicity for Reiki not only benefits the person concerned but the Reiki community as a whole.

Television

Television is another great medium for free exposure. One way to get free exposure is to target lifestyle programmes. In particular, programmes which are dedicated to health, lifestyle, or wellness. You may even get a chance to appear on travel programmes, if the programme is looking at things to do when they feature your town.

Simply pick up a copy of the local television guide and see which programmes your service may fall into. All you need to do is call the Television stations, to see if they are interested in doing a segment on Reiki. You will get plenty of knock backs, but you have nothing to lose if you receive only one 'yes'.

Another alternative is to fax a press release to television stations. Give the station an overview of what you offer and how this may be of interest to the audience of the programme concerned.

Lifestyle programmes which are scheduled for prime time viewing are also worthy of consideration. You don't want to be on television at 3am, along with the shopping channels. So it is best to try for programmes scheduled between 5pm and 9pm.

You may also consider a spot on the evening news, or a small feature in a current affairs programme, but be sure the producer does not turn your complementary therapy into a weird 'spiritual thing'. I have witnessed this several times. One example was a short piece on T.M. (Transcendental Meditation).

The initial interview was fine, as I knew the person concerned but prior to airing, the producer decided to sensationalize the interview. They added unrelated footage of strange looking meditation Yogi's from

India and added music by Pink Floyd. The overall effect made it look like some kind of bizarre cult, which of course it is not, but the damage had already been done.

But as they say, publicity, be it good or bad, is better than none at all.

Direct point of sale
In addition to your usual means of promotion it may also be worth considering utilizing other direct ways to promote your business.

Some examples might include: Bumper Stickers, Fridge Magnets, Car Magnets, Postcards and Book Marks.

It can be relatively inexpensive to produce these additional tools of promotion.

Let us take a look at these one by one:

Bumper Stickers
Bumper stickers are great 'give away' items to give your existing clients or anyone else who makes an enquiry. You would be surprised just how many people actually use bumper stickers, not just on their cars but in other places too.

Fridge Magnets
Fridge Magnets are another popular way to be remembered. Why not turn your business card into a fridge magnet? I have visited friends over the years and have seen fridge magnet business cards on their fridge, remaining year after year. Let's face it, who doesn't meditate daily on their fridge?

Car Magnets
Car Magnets are also recommended but you should choose a colour scheme to match your car or alternatively, create a colour scheme for your business logo which matches your current car. It also makes sense that you are willing to draw attention to your car. If your current car's next trip is to the car wreckers, you might be better off skipping on the car magnet option, for cosmetic reasons.

Postcards and Book Marks
Creating a free postcard is another great idea and is a promotional tool that others will mail around the world for you. Be sure to make your postcard attractive, relevant and eye catching. In the same way that you

would buy a postcard as a tourist, so you should make your postcard design appealing, witty or engaging. Most important of all, make it relate to your business or service in some way.

If you wish to make a book mark, use it as an advertising tool. Remember to use the front and back of the book mark and remember the saying, 'the more you tell, the more you sell'. Why not write a short story about Reiki with an engaging headline. More often than not, people will read it, as curiosity will get the better of them.

With all of the previously mentioned mediums, remember to spare no expense on the layout and design. If you do not have these skills *(and I mean honestly)* then go the distance and employ the skills of a graphic designer. Also, pay careful attention to what you wish to say. You need to clearly sell yourself or your service in an interesting way.

Expos, Psychic Fairs and Competitions

These days, there are a variety of expos for 'mind, body and spirit', health, spiritual, and psychic fairs. These events are a prime location to promote your Reiki practice. If you intend to participate in an expo and obtain a stall to offer treatments, you will need to consider just how many new clients you will need to obtain as a direct result, in order to pay for the stall. To ensure you cover costs and generate new clients, it is essential to give expo visitors a special offer to secure future bookings. Another great way to build up your future clientele is to run a competition.

An example might be where expo visitors fill out a coupon to be in the running for a series of three free Reiki treatments or some other prize of your choice. In the meantime, you will have obtained numerous phone numbers, addresses and email addresses to notify all those who did not win on a follow-up offer. For example you might write a letter or send an email along the following lines:

> "Dear...
>
> *I am writing this email to thank you for participating in our 'win 3 free Reiki treatments competition'. Unfortunately, your name was not drawn for the major prize however, as a consolation, I would like to offer you a 'Buy one, get one free trial offer'. If you make a booking before (Date of your choosing) you can take advantage of this 'not to be missed' special offer. Simply phone....to make a booking.*

Please also find enclosed some information about Reiki as well as some testimonials from previous clients who benefitted from my service.

I look forward to hearing from you at your nearest opportunity.

Signed, (your name).

Running a competition and sending out letters or emails in this manner can really add new clients to your practice and competition participants will also appreciate being offered a consolation prize.

Advertising on Mailing Lists

If you have the opportunity to obtain access to other peoples' mailing lists or newsletters, this is yet another way to expand your client base.

This might take the form of an advertisement in a newsletter, or arranging to have someone of standing recommend your services. This not only adds new clients, it adds credibility to yourself as a recognized practitioner.

If you already have an established mailing list, you might use this as a means to swap lists with another practitioner, thus forming a strategic alliance.

10
Advertising: Best Kept Secrets

The common Advertising pitfalls
Advertising is one of those things that you can spend an awful lot of money on with little or no response, if you fail to follow proven strategies for success. The tragedy is that many practitioners have no idea how to advertise themselves and continue to advertise every week, or monthly for years, hoping that just having their name in the market place will eventually bring in new clientele. Unfortunately for the most part, this waiting game can land you with empty pockets in no time at all.

The good news is that in this chapter you will find indispensable tools which will not only save you hundreds of dollars but will dramatically bring in new clients.

Before I illustrate how to create advertising that generates enquiries and bookings, let's look at some of the more common myths about advertising so that you may better avoid these in your dealings.

Myth #1 Bigger is better
Although a bigger ad will often draw more attention, it may not translate into business unless you know how to sell yourself. Over the years I have seen that small space ads can be just as effective, if not more than one big advertisement. Bigger is not always favourable and if you are advertising in press or magazine publications, you can spend a lot of money for little results. Of course, advertisers will tell you that a bigger ad will generate more sales, but that is what they are trained to tell you. To sell more advertising space is the main aim of most magazines and newspapers.

Myth #2 Repetition
Another common advertising myth is that of repetition. Many sales

people will tell you that it is enough to keep putting your name out there month after month, year after year, as eventually people will notice your advertising. For the most part they will notice your advertising but will not necessarily act upon it. The fact of the matter is not how many times your advertisement is repeated but the content of the advertising which counts. One ad can generate hundreds of calls over another, depending upon the content. You have to check what you are saying and if it is not working, you need to change it. Holding out on the thought that by the third or fourth month, people will see your ad is costly and so many people do this month after month with little results.

Myth #3 Ads should look like Ads
Another common myth is that your ad should look like an ad. When I read a magazine, I want to read the magazine for its articles. I don't buy a magazine to read the ads.

When you create your ad to look like an article in the magazine, you will guarantee readership and ultimately greater sales.

Myth #4 Cosmetic Ads sell
Another common advertising pitfall is that your ads appearance should look cosmetic or fancy. The use of full colour, high definition artistic photography and little copy may work for Coke or Sony but you aren't a global corporation with decades of product branding to be instantly recognized. It can be the case that when your ad looks too polished, people will simply gloss over it, thinking that whatever you're offering is too expensive.

Myth #5 Getting your name out there is enough
Will maintaining your advertisement in the same place in a magazine or newspaper guarantee sales? Unfortunately, this is not true. Unless you are offering something which will flag down your readers interest or entice them to find out more, your name in the market place is not enough. Magazines and newspapers will hold you in the greatest esteem but your wallet will shrink. You need to advertise with intelligence and produce ads that work.

Myth #6 Too much copy, drops readership
Another advertising myth is that if you put too much information into an advertisement, no one will read the copy. The truth of the matter is

that nothing could be further from the truth. In fact, the more you tell, the more you sell. Even if you are doing a small classified ad that only costs you a few dollars every month, you can offer your readers access to information via your website or offer them a free information pack in the mail. Your future clients want to know what's in it for them, so your free information kit is a way to persuade them to use your service.

How to create winning ads
The secret to creating winning ads is to produce ads that offer solutions to peoples problems. The first thing you need to determine is 'why do people come for Reiki treatments?' One simple way to find this out is to ask. Ask people you know who have received a treatment in the past and ask people who have not. This is also a great way to renew old clients as well as generating new clients who may be interested by trying a session. The idea of a survey is to ask at least 50 people, and ideally 100 or more. Think of the level of business you will drum up just by doing this exercise.

Offer solutions to their problems
Having conducted this exercise, you might find that some of the more common responses to the question include:

- Feeling out of balance
- Feeling tired
- Emotionally drained or going through emotional problems
- To heal a specific injury or various aches and pains.

These are but a few of the common responses you will encounter. Now you need to wrap these reasons into a definitive statement which provides a solution to their problems.
　Here are some headlines to get you started.

> *Feeling tired and out of balance? In just 30 minutes Reiki brings you back into balance.*
> *Discover the seven secrets to renewed health and vitality in minutes. Details call…. (visit: www.yourwebsite.com) etc…*
> *Energy crisis? Reiki renews your vital energy. For more information call…..*
> *Are you sick and tired of feeling sick and tired? Reiki is a gentle, safe*

and non invasive hands-on healing touch therapy which renews your vital energy and brings a deeply relaxing experience in just minutes…. For more information call…..

Advertising which says – 'what's in it for them'

When you write an ad for Reiki, you need to identify with your clients problem, and offer them a solution. You also need to convince them that they will get value for parting with their hard earned money. One of the best ways to do this is to remove risk from the equation and list benefits, not just features.

Benefits versus features

Benefits represent the motivating results of a Reiki treatment. These might include: relief from pain, renewed vitality, and restful sleep. Other benefits might include: spiritual development, better quality of life, improved self-esteem, and greater happiness.

Features on the other hand are less important, which might include: the latest massage table for treatments, easy parking out the front of your therapy room, friendly customer service, clinic location etc. Although these features add credibility to your practice they are not the motivating factors for choosing you over another practitioner.

In terms of your advertising, the benefits are what you need to put in front of your clients, as these are the motivating forces which will turn your enquiry into a booking.

Words to use, words to avoid

The words you choose for your advertising have a large impact on the results.

The following are words to use which are engaging for readers:

- free
- easy
- guarantee
- results
- proven
- safe
- save money
- you/your
- discover

- health
- love
- new
- value
- free gift
- buy one, get one free.
- 50% off
- half price

The following words are strong words that sell:

- comfort
- deserve
- happy
- fun
- instant
- now
- person's name
- you've won!
- profit
- proud
- trust
- benefit

The following is an example of a headline which incorporates some of these motivating words for your advertising.

"Discover the new, safe, and proven way to enjoy renewed health and vitality with Reiki. Results are guaranteed or it's free!"

The following words are to be avoided where possible.

- bad
- contract
- cost
- deal
- death
- difficult
- failure
- hurt
- liability

- loss
- lose
- obligation
- pay
- price
- sign
- maybe
- hard
- decline

Call to action

Creating a deadline to your advertising creates urgency, which is a powerfully motivating factor when you want your customers to do it now. We all know how it is when we have all the time in the world to do something. Time goes by and the next thing we know, we have forgotten all about it.

When you call people to action, with an enticing offer like your ½ price treatments are limited to the first 10 callers, you will be surprised just how quickly the phone rings.

When you tell your client to act, in more cases than not, they do. An example which calls your client to action might be:

"Call before March 24th to receive your free gift, no questions asked"

Your limited offer which is valid for the next 7 days, may be in reality your on-going offer, but for someone who sees your advertisement or classified ad for the first time, it is an opportunity not to be missed.

Of course, you need to keep your offers fresh and to change them regularly, so as not to seem like your 'one week only' special offer is actually every week (even though this might be the case). The idea is to mix things up, to keep your offers fresh for new and old readers too.

Test your advertising

In any form of advertising, it is vitally important that you test your ad on a regular basis. When you place a new ad in a magazine, be sure that you have the option in the booking contract to make changes to the ad before the next issue.

Some people spend thousands of dollars every month, or worse, every week on ads that do not bring in enquiries, let alone sales. If you place an ad and you do not get a response, change your ad as soon as possible, unless you have money to burn. It is important to monitor your enquiries and if you have none, change what you are doing immediately.

When you do receive calls, (especially if you have advertised in more than one place), always ask the person where they saw your ad or how they heard about you. This way you will know which ad worked and which medium drew the most enquiries. Keep a tally of the number of calls made and from where. Also tally email enquiries or enquiries made from referrals or word of mouth. Within a short period of time you will be able to see which format is most effective for your business.

Once you have found a form of advertising that works, and continues to work, keep on doing the same thing until you notice a dramatic change. Not all advertising works well forever so continual monitoring is essential to the success of your business.

Creative copy writing

When you write the copy for your ads, it is best to write in a manner which is authentic and uncontrived. One recommendation is to write your ads like you speak. Imagine you are at a party and someone asks you what you do for a living. Rather than saying: *"I do Reiki"* trying saying it like this. *"You know how people get stressed out from overwork and not enough rest, well I offer a natural way to re-energize their body and mind by transferring vital life force energy from my hands into their body. Its called Reiki, have you heard of it before?"*

Now isn't that more interesting and engaging than: *"I do Reiki"*.

The trick to any good copywriting is to present what you offer in a personal and easy to understand way, so that your reader can directly relate to what you are saying. If you can make an emotional connection to your reader, you capture their immediate interest.

When it comes to writing the copy for your brochures or advertising, there are several things to avoid. Some of these include the use of puns or clichés.

For example: *"Come for healing to bring back that heavenly feeling"*, or;

"It's our birthday, but you get the presents", or;

"We're the best in the west"

Groan! Shall I stop now?

Other things to avoid are putting your copy in CAPITAL LETTERS. CAPITAL LETTERS ARE FINE IN MOST CASES FOR HEADLINES BUT IF YOU USE CAPITAL LETTERS FOR YOUR COPY IT IS MORE DIFFICULT FOR THE READER TO GET THROUGH THE TEXT.

Another thing to consider is the use of fonts (typeface).

If you choose a font which is hard to read, you will lose your reader because it will become too much work on the eyes to continue reading. In general, script fonts are not recommended and can be hard on the reader at the best of times.

It is also recommended to use a serif font as apposed to a **Sans-serif** font. Serif fonts have the little tails on the top and bottom of the letters which make then generally easier to read.

Whereas Sans-serif fonts do not have the tails and this can make reading body copy harder on the eye.

It is also not recommended to use type faces which are too **narrow**, as again the reader will have to work too hard to read the copy and likewise a typeface that is too wide will again have a less than desired effect.

Some people also like to use unusual type faces for their body copy but this too can be hard work for the reader.

Some of these fonts are best suited for party invitations but are not necessarily useful for general copy. If you want to make a point in your copy then there are things which work and others which don't.

If you want to make a section of your copy to stand out, then make it bold.

This highlights the section and naturally draws the reader's eye to that point.

The use of underlining copy on the other hand is not recommended for copy as this again makes the reader labour through the text and interferes with the otherwise easy to read feel of text without underlines. Isn't that better?

Another point to mention is the use of bullets to draw the reader's eye to important points. Bullets are also great for giving the reader a summary of the points we are wishing to make.

Bullets:

- Make a point
- Will make your point stand out
- Help the reader get your point
- And gives an overall impression in…
- Point form.

11
Free Publicity

The only thing that is worse than being talked about by others is not being talked about at all. When it comes to your Reiki practice, if you can get people talking about you and what you offer, then your business will prosper. The following are some proven ways of creating publicity and increasing your public profile.

Writing Articles

One excellent way to gain exposure is through writing articles on your practice and having these published through local newspapers, new-age or holistic magazines and the internet. Most magazines and newspapers are always looking for a feature article about a diverse array of subjects.

Writing an article on Reiki can boost your public profile as well as increasing public awareness of Reiki. Every time an article is written and published on Reiki, every Reiki practitioner and teacher wins. If you find another practitioner who has had an article published on Reiki, don't feel like you have missed the boat, they have done you and Reiki an enormous service.

You can be a part of this by putting your fingers to work on the keyboard, or pen to paper and getting your message out to the masses. You will be amazed how a simple article will bring in a torrent of new clients from all walks of life.

Giving Talks

Giving public talks on Reiki is another way to increase your clientele and profile. Try your local community centre, bookshop, healing centre or new-age shop. Offer an information evening about Reiki and its benefits. If you are offering a talk at one of these venues, often they will promote your talk free of charge and this alone promotes your services to the wider community. The best way to get the numbers is to offer the talk free of charge. You might also look into some small notices in the local paper to get the word out. If you are offering a free talk, some papers may offer a free advertisement by mentioning you in the 'what's happening' section.

When preparing your talk, be sure that you practice what you wish to say beforehand. Preparation is the key to giving a successful talk.

You may also consider reading some books on public speaking, or do a short course on the subject to fine tune your presentation skills.

One way to structure a talk on Reiki may include some of the following points:

- An introduction of yourself and your background and experience in Reiki
- An overview of what you will be talking about
- The origins and history of Reiki
- How someone becomes a channel of Reiki
- The Reiki attunements and the Reiki Lineage
- How a treatment is given
- The benefits of a Reiki treatment
- Give a short demonstration and treatment, explaining what you are doing.
- Guide a short Reiki meditation
- Finish with question and answer time
- Give out your contact details and a special offer for follow up treatments

Once you have given your talk, you can also offer up people further information by mail or email, as well as calling them for feedback in regards to your talk. All they have to do is give their contact details for you to follow up.

Putting on a Fundraising Event

Another way to increase public awareness is to put on a fund-raising event or raffle in conjunction with a non-profit charitable organization. This could be a charitable ball, a raffle which includes your services as a prize, or some other form of publicity to increase your exposure as a practitioner of Reiki.

Riding on the back of other well known charities is a great way to give your practice an enormous boost because many have the resources and funding to aid you in achieving your goals.

12

The Lifetime value of a Client

Why existing clients are so valuable

Many people underestimate the lifetime value of their clients and once they have received one booking, they are forever striving to obtain new clients. As you may be aware, it is far easier to sell a second time to an existing client than it is to find a new one. The main reason for this is that your existing client already knows you and your service. Provided you offered a service of value, you can be sure that your existing client will buy again if you ask them to. Once you have secured a new client and have given them a treatment, you really should bend over backwards to keep them happy with your service because if they are happy, they will use your service not only again but several times and may tell many of their friends, who will also use your service in the future.

When you think about it, one treatment can translate into dozens, just by providing excellent customer service and offering incentives to return or tell their friends.

No other form of advertising works better than word of mouth and to not utilize this golden opportunity with your existing clients will lose you on-going business.

In summary, the reasons an existing client is valuable:

1. **Already converted**. Meaning they are sold on the benefits of what you can offer, through direct experience.
2. **Repeat Business.** They will bring in repeat business (provided they are happy with your sessions) by re-booking a treatment in the future.
3. **Will tell their friends.** The most important of all three. If your treatments shine, they will invariably refer you to their friends and family members.

Following on from the third point, why not encourage your new clients to actively tell people about your services. One way to do this is to give your client 5 of your business cards. Tell them, *"Most of my advertising is via word of mouth, so if you enjoyed your treatment, then please pass these on to some of your friends, who you think might benefit as well."*

Another thing you can do is give them an incentive. For example, you might offer them a 10% discount off their next treatment for every time they directly refer you a new client. Tell them to tell their friends to say *"(Your client's name) was the one who told me about your treatments"*. Alternatively, offer your client a free gift in the post and thank them for referring new people to you. They will not only be surprised to receive a formal thank you, they will genuinely feel appreciated and this will invariably secure future appointments as well as on-going referrals.

How to rekindle old clients

Its takes time and money to acquire new clients and although some remain, others fall by the wayside after one or more treatments overtime. The important thing to consider here is that you have already sold them on the benefits of your service and all you need to do is ensure that they will want to use your service in the future.

The following are some additional ways which will help you rekindle the smouldering ambers of yesterday's clients, into renewed ones.

Keep in touch every 90 days

Have you ever wondered why advertisers promote their product or service not once but several times? Keeping your service in front of your existing clients at least every 90 days, reminds them that you still exist and that they should consider your services in the future. This can be easily achieved in one of the following ways:

Newsletters and Special Offers

Offer your existing clients a regular mail-out, be this a special offer for your treatments, or a discount for their birthday. By putting your name in front of them, you become memorable and entice them to use your service once again.

If you have a large client base, you may consider a regular e-newsletter. This will save you time and money when it comes to stuffing envelopes and postage, as you can simply compile email groups and send these out in the hundreds, with just one click.

Preferred client club – VIP Membership

Another way to encourage old clients is to offer them free VIP membership for preferred clients. As a part of this club, they are entitled to a free gift such as a 'two for one' offer.

VIP membership will make your client feel special and even taken aback that you consider them a VIP. You might even go to the trouble of making a VIP preferred customer laminated card.

Ask them to buy

In all of your promotional material, always ask your client to buy. This should be stated at the beginning of your letter, repeated again in the middle and finally repeated again at the end of the letter.

An example might be: *"Dear (clients name) I am writing this email/ letter to bring to your attention that you have qualified for a Free 1 hour Reiki Treatment to the value of ($.....) To take advantage of this free gift, simply book a 1 hour Reiki treatment before (June 30th) and your next treatment is Free. Call now to claim your free gift."*

Exceptional Customer Service

If you want to maintain the life-time value of your client you need to offer not just customer service, but *exceptional* customer service.

When speaking with your clients over the phone, be friendly and polite and do your best to deliver the best possible service you can.

When returning calls, do your upmost to return missed calls the same day, if not within the same hour the call was made.

If you are going to post your enquirer some information, over deliver on your promises. If you say that you will mail them some information on a Monday, tell them that they will receive it Wednesday. To ensure you over deliver, make certain that they receive it a day before they expect it. When you get what you want, faster than you expect, it leaves you pleasantly surprised and satisfied with the service being offered.

When your client arrives for their treatment, offer them a drink (preferably water) and engage in some small chat*, asking them how they are or what they have been doing.

This not only keeps things personal, it tells your client that you are

---

* One word of caution here is not to allow the chat time to go on for too long, as this will cut into your session time and the amount of time they have for the treatment.

interested in them as a person, not just as a client.

Another thing you can do every now and then is go over time, or offer a free gift at the end of the treatment. It need not be a big gift, just something small, or even a compliment. This can give your client an added boost and they will love you for that.

The Power of Thank you

Remember what your mother told you about please and thank you? Manners are important and by saying thanks at the end of your treatment, you really honour the person. Always thank your client at the end of the treatment, for they are doing you a service just by being there. They offer you a valuable chance to refine and practice your healing abilities, they are also paying you for that opportunity, so say thanks and they will feel valued and respected.

Another thing you might consider is to offer your existing clients a thank you card in the mail, or an e-card over the internet. Again, this need not be a big deal, just a little note to say thank you for their patronage. This is especially important on birthdays and Christmas. You can obtain your clients' birthday dates when you obtain their client history, in your initial interview prior to your first treatment. When your client receives a card on their birthday, they will be left feeling valued, that you made the effort to acknowledge them.

Another important point to make is that of remembering your client's name. Nothing is as de-valuing as forgetting a clients name or worse, calling them the wrong name. This includes making sure your client's name is spelt correctly when sending promotional materials. Whether these are letters or email correspondence, personalize where possible. It is also better to send out individual emails to your client list rather than bulk email. Always write or email: *Dear (clients' name)* not *Dear Sir/Madam* or *Valued Customer*. Otherwise is just looks like spam and lacks the personal touch.

The benefit of feedback

One of the most valuable things your clients can give you is constructive feedback. Never miss an opportunity to learn how you can improve the service you are offering.

One simple idea is to give your client a quick feedback sheet at the end of your session. Ask them if they wouldn't mind spending a minute to complete the tick box questionnaire.

Here's an example you may wish to use in your treatments.

"I/We value your comments and feedback. Please take a moment to complete this form. Your comments will be kept strictly confidential."

1. How would you rate your overall experience?
   Poor / Average / Good / Very Good / Excellent
2. Did you feel this treatment represented value for money? **Yes / No**
3. Would you recommend our treatments to others? **Yes / No**
4. Did this treatment meet your expectations? **Yes / No**
5. What did you like most about this treatment?

_____
_____
_____
_____

6. What do you feel could be improved?

_____
_____
_____
_____

7. Other comments or suggestions?

_____
_____
_____
_____

Name: _____
Contact Number: _____ Email: _____

This feedback sheet is only a guide and you may wish to make changes to suit your treatments.

Once you have received several feedback sheets of this kind, you will start to see where your business can be improved and make changes accordingly.

Another way to obtain feedback is to mail or email this feedback form to your clients or post it with a postage paid self addressed envelope so all they need to do is complete the form and post it back at no cost to them.

Following up on constructive criticism and being accountable

If you truly wish to make your service of healing others the best it can be, then it makes sense to know what others think about what you do. When you obtain any feedback you should be more interested in what can be improved, than what is good about your service. Although it is nice to hear how much someone loved your session, it does not really help you to improve your service. What you really need to know is what is wrong with your service and then be able to take steps to improve it. When you receive constructive criticism, don't take it personally, just take the necessary steps to improve your service. No one is perfect, and we can always learn something new.

13
Networking your Business

Every time you meet someone new, it is an opportunity to network your business. This does not need to be aggressive networking which many people resent, especially if they are being canvassed to join a Network Marketing Company or MLM (Multi-level Marketing). In all but a few cases when you meet someone new, people will eventually come to the question of what you do for a living. This can be an opportunity to explain what you do, including how it can benefit people and more importantly, them. The thing is, you never know just how often you will encounter an opportunity to network your business and this is why you should always have at least a few business cards handy. As I have explained before, your business card is your mini brochure, so always have some handy. Never try to force a card on someone, if the interest is present, give them two cards, saying something like: *"If you like I'll give you my card* (giving them two or three) *and if you know someone who might benefit from what I do, feel free to pass it on."*

Forming a strategic alliance
Another way to increase your business is to form a strategic alliance, which can be really easy and very rewarding. This is where you form an agreement between yourself and another practitioner.

Once you have done this successfully, there is no limit to the number of therapists you can extend this to. I myself have used this system well in the past and have a network of over 30 therapists, I refer to and from whom I am referred, on a regular basis.

The thing with strategic alliances is that you need to be sure it is reciprocal, so the best way to test the waters for a time is to always ask who it was that referred you. Once you know the alliance is a two way agreement in practice, you have a 'win, win' scenario for all concerned.

Referral rewards program

A further extension of the strategic alliance is to offer a rewards program. This is where you offer Reiki treatments or some other goods and services to those who are actively referring new clients your way. Not unlike the reward systems that many airlines are using, as well as credit card providers, you can reward those who refer you or utilize your services on an on-going basis.

Get creative on this point, as it is fast becoming a trend in our modern world. It has worked well for others, so why not get on board and ride the wave.

Expanding your client base

In order to reach a wider audience with Reiki, it's important to think outside the scope of what is considered normal forms of advertising. There are many places where Reiki can be of benefit and the following are some additional suggestion where you can not only source new clients, but where you can extend your practice to the wider community.

Schools, Universities and Colleges

Why not contact your local School or University? You could offer Reiki treatments to stressed out exam students, or teachers who need time out from stressed out students. Many schools and universities have notice boards and these are ideal places to advertise your services. Today, many younger people have a deep interest in healing and spirituality and you have an opportunity to obtain new clients by advertising in this largely untapped market.

Beauty Therapists, Day Spas, and Health Retreats

Beauty therapy centres, day spas and health retreats offer massage as well as many other forms of relaxation therapy, so why not offer your services as a practitioner? You may find that you will be able to gain a part-time position giving treatments and the benefit is that the centre will arrange your bookings and will have a suitable room for giving your sessions. Although you will not be paid at your usual rate, you will benefit from a regular clientele.

Sports and Recreation Centres

Another largely untapped market is your local sports and recreation centre. Here your Reiki treatments can be advertised as assisting with the treatment of sports injury and increasing vitality, as well as enhancing overall performance levels. Much in the same way that sports massage is utilized, Reiki can be an ideal partner therapy.

14
Getting Professional

There are a number of ways to increase your clientele, but perhaps the most important is to strive to further your knowledge and skills through regular Reiki practice as well as upgrading your Reiki training. If we pay little attention to our personal and professional development, it matters little that we have all of the best marketing and advertising skills, if the service we offer is less than credible. We therefore need to be a living example of what we practice and be vigilant in working not only on our professional presentation, but our self-healing and spiritual development as well.

By working closely with our Reiki teacher and attending regular Reiki reviews, we can do much to increase our experience and knowledge of Reiki. It is also advisable to continue Reiki training to higher levels and thus, further our skills with new methods and experience.

Ultimately, the practice of Reiki is the greatest teacher. The more you do, the more you become. Practice makes perfect or at least more perfect, day by day.

Reiki Associations

In addition to regular Reiki practice and upgrading your Reiki training, it is also advisable to be affiliated with Reiki organizations, associations and institutes. The internet is a wonderful resource when it comes to finding Reiki associations. Simply type 'Reiki Associations' in a search engine, such as www.google.com and you will find a number to choose from. The International Institute for Reiki Training also offers Associate membership world-wide and you can find out more information by visiting our website at: www.reikitraining.com.au

Practitioner Insurance

If you are serious about your Reiki practice then it is also advisable and sometimes mandatory to obtain Practitioner Insurance. Many associations now offer Practitioner Insurance as part of their membership benefits. Namely, one should obtain insurance which protects you for Public Liability and Professional Risk.

In a nutshell, Public Liability means that if, whilst receiving a treatment (for example on your premises), a client injures themselves, then you are covered.

Professional Indemnity covers all professional risk. This means that if, for some reason, the person you are treating is injured as a direct result of your treatment, or claims this to be the case, you are also covered.

Although many would scoff at the very notion that you could harm anyone with Reiki, one needs to be aware that there are those who might make such claims against practitioners. Although the risk is low, it is still worth insuring, all things considered.

If you are operating from a premises such as a health centre, or from your own home, it is worth considering public liability insurance. Although Reiki is one of the safest healing arts imaginable and we'd like to think that nothing could go wrong whilst giving a treatment, there is always the possibility of an accident or incident which may potentially compromise your practice.

Besides insurance, it is also in ones best interest to be conscious of any preventative measures which may avoid accidents happening.

If you operate out of premises, be sure to check the environment for any accidents waiting to happen. For example, a loose carpet, an unsafe treatment table, slippery floors or power cords in the path of people in high traffic areas. Keeping a safe workplace is a simple task of assessing your environment and making conscious changes where needed.

Today there are many insurance companies which now insure practitioners and teachers of Reiki. When looking for practitioner insurance, be sure to get a number of quotes and to make sure the insurance company understands what you are offering. You will find that prices vary from a few hundred dollars to thousands, so it is worth shopping around for the best quote to suit your practice.

The following two websites offer Practitioner Insurance for Reiki Practitioners and Teachers as well as other Complementary Therapists: visit www.reikitraining.com.au or www.iict.com.au

Section Two
Reiki Sensei
The Art of Teaching Reiki

Introduction to Section Two: Reiki Sensei – The Art of Teaching Reiki

Section Two of *The Ultimate Reiki Guide for Practitioners and Masters* focusses on the path to teaching Reiki. Commonly referred to as the Reiki Masters level, this level of practice *(for it is a practice)* is a guide to passing on the teachings of Reiki to others.

When I recall my own decision to commence Reiki Master teacher training, it set in motion a whole new level of personal growth and inner awakening, not to mention a certain amount of personal struggle, both emotional and mental.

When I commenced my teacher training, some 12 years ago, there was very little information available in books pertaining to how one became a teacher of Reiki. Much of my personal discovery of this process occurred through direct experience. I took it upon myself to attend dozens of Reiki seminars in a variety of styles, in order to extend my personal experience of the practice of Reiki. I also asked my initiating teachers *(much to their credit and constant patience)* a great deal of questions. It was through this on-going search for information, practice and direct experience that Reiki shaped who I am today.

With the enormous popularity of Reiki throughout the Western World over the last 30 years, there have been many books published on learning Reiki from the point of view of a practitioner, yet little information has been published on the subject of teaching Reiki. It is for this reason that I have decided to set down in writing some of the guidelines to being a teacher of Reiki.

In addition to the general guidelines of teaching Reiki, I have also added a section on dispelling some of the common limitations which have been placed on the system of Reiki. I call these the myths of Reiki.

It is hoped that section two of this book will guide you in the Art of Teaching Reiki. May you be guided in making these ways available to your own students and help to develop the muilt-faceted experience which is Reiki.

Lawrence Ellyard

15

Starting on the Teacher's path

Beginning the path of a Reiki teacher is the start of a new and exciting journey. It is a journey of self-discovery, healing, service and sharing the gentle art of healing with others. To teach Reiki is to become an instrument of the Divine. It is a path which commands humility and service. There is no room for self-grandeur or sitting high upon a pedestal. Through the process of initiation, we become the conduit between the Universal energy and the person being attuned.

When we commence this journey of self-discovery, we need to consider why we wish to walk this path. Some seek the higher levels purely for an increase in personal growth and self-healing. Others come to the teaching level with a strong desire to pass the practice of Reiki onto others. Others still, practice with the intention of increasing their spiritual development with Reiki.

When we start upon the teacher's path, in many respects, it is to follow a calling.

This 'calling' occurs throughout many healing traditions. In the same way that a priest is called to the priesthood, a monk to be initiated in a Buddhist order or a shaman is called by means of a near death experience, a powerful dream, a vision or illness, so practitioners of Reiki are called to be teachers.

Being called is not necessarily a booming voice from the heavens, saying *"You are chosen to teach Reiki"*, though I have heard of such cases. More often, the call comes in many subtle ways.

When we examine how people came to Reiki, it is usually a combination of an internal knowing, followed by an outer prompting from the Universe. This can manifest in the form of an illness, crisis, a chance meeting, dreams, a vision or by simply recognising that the Universe is holding up a big flashing neon sign, pointing you upon the teacher's path.

Whichever way the call comes, if one has made certain promises on a karmic level, then those who are meant to be teachers are guided by Reiki and the journey begins.

Reiki has a way of tapping practitioners on the shoulder. When there is a strong karmic connection to healing and teaching others, the Reiki energy will make itself known.

Becoming a teacher of Reiki is not just a nice thing to do over a weekend, it represents a life transition and for many, a life path. Provided you have met an authentic teacher of the Reiki tradition who has a stable and unbroken transmission of the Reiki teachings, the path of passing on your teacher's tradition can be profound and deeply moving.

Even if someone comes to be teaching Reiki without a clear understanding of this inner process, by simply practicing and teaching others, this will become more and more apparent as time and classes go by.

Who should teach Reiki and what are the pre-requisites?

Since Reiki has become increasingly popular in the West, many people have embraced Reiki teachings for the simple, yet effective methods of transformation and healing. However, with this tremendous interest, the ability to find genuine teachers with authentic training is hard. Reiki is a Lineage-based tradition and therefore it is vitally important that those who teach it, not only know what they are doing, they must also have true and unbroken transmissions of the Reiki lineage.

Much like lighting a candle from one person to another, the transmission which is given via the attunements must be passed correctly, in order for the flame to continue. Therefore, it is incumbent upon the teacher of Reiki, if they choose this path, to make certain that what they are offering is authentic and true to the best of their knowledge.

If we think of this analogy of passing one candle flame to another, we need to be sure our candles are good and burn well. Mikao Usui was the first candle and his flame burned brightly. He passed his teachings to his students who, in turn, passed on the Reiki fire to their students and so forth. With every generation, the flame is passed.

Reiki has also been referred to as a 'Chinese Whisper' or rather a 'Japanese Whisper' as the origins of the system suggest.

As the system of Reiki is passed down, from one generation of teachers to the next, it is common that things will change. Each teacher flavours their practice of Reiki to make it their own. However, when it comes to the teachings, it is important that the methods and attunements are not changed to the point of becoming something entirely different from that of their teacher's system.

This dilution of information occurs when a teacher significantly changes the content of the information received from their teacher and more directly, when a teacher adds their own methods, calling them the original teachings, without making clear distinctions between what is and isn't traditional Reiki.

To be a teacher, one needs direct personal experience of what will be taught. It goes without saying that the path of a teacher first requires considerable experience as a practitioner of Reiki. For one cannot teach about what one has not understood.

It is for this reason that it is considered important to have completed several months of practice in the beginner and intermediate levels or better still, years, before considering the path of teaching Reiki.

Sadly, the old traditions and such virtues as patience and long-term dedication can often be overlooked in our eagerness and desire for instant gratification and titles like 'Reiki Master'. Maybe it is our western "quick fix" mind set. But, like many traditions, one does not achieve noticeable results without dedication to the practices and the requisite qualities of right intention and humility.

One of the best ways to learn how to teach Reiki is by participation in a number of Reiki seminars, where the teacher in training, by observing, (and later teaching) gains understanding under the guidance and supervision of their Reiki teacher. This serves as an excellent training ground for developing what it means to teach Reiki.

To become a teacher of Reiki there are three key points for preparation.

These are: practice; healing oneself; and healing others.

It makes sense that if we are to become experienced in the practice of Reiki, that practice is the bedrock of teaching others. Regular attendance to one's personal healing is paramount. One should also consider distant healing on oneself as a daily practice. The daily application of distant healing and self-healing is a great way to remove personal obstacles to our healing.

The other necessary practice is that of healing others. One should, where possible, attend to this by offering healing sessions to family and friends. One does not necessarily have to rely on paying clients to participate in gaining experience. Whether we are working on the terminally ill or a headache, each healing session brings a wealth of experience and greater understanding of Reiki.

Finding the right teacher and what to look for

Hopefully, if you are reading this book, you have already encountered a Reiki teacher of reputable standing and therefore have found a teacher in whom you have confidence to teach you the higher levels. If, on the other hand you have not, you need to seek out a qualified teacher.

When finding a teacher, one of the main obstacles is ourselves. Often with our eagerness to learn it all, it is vitally important to approach this first step with patience and humility. As the saying goes, *"When the student is ready the teacher appears."* It is therefore important to note that once a student has finally found their teacher and has made a firm commitment to begin their journey to Reiki Mastery, it is quite common for certain issues of self-doubt to arise. This can lead to 'Ego struggles', which sometimes means: *"When the teacher is ready, the student disappears".*

Although this is said in jest, to a degree it can happen. It is often the case that when we finally find what we have been seeking, our issues of self-sabotage tend to appear. The thing to remember is that when obstacles arise, we have an opportunity to work with them. Most of the time is it about ourselves, our own healing and the choice to transform, or run away.

When looking for a suitable teacher, there are a number of qualities to look for.

Keep in mind that you may have to wait for the right teacher, so it is important not to let convenience or money be the only deciding factors. It can really be a mistake to look for the cheapest Reiki Master class in town, as you often get what you pay for.

When we are investing in our spiritual lives and personal well-being, it makes sense to research a teacher well, and not rush in blindly, because of the 'quick fix, instant enlightenment' mentality. Stepping upon the spiritual path can be really exciting and people may embrace everything with such enthusiasm, yet they often discard ideals like common sense and discernment. These ideals are very important, so check yourself and check your teachers.

Following is a general guide to finding a suitable teacher and what to look for:

1. Check the teacher's Reiki lineage. They should be able to tell you who they learnt from and their Reiki Lineage dating back to the founding teacher, Mikao Usui. Some Reiki lineages are many legs long and may be watered down significantly by distorted views and insufficient training from their initiating instructor.
2. Ask how long they have been teaching Reiki and for how long their teacher was training. Do they teach Reiki regularly and do they use Reiki on themselves and others daily?
3. Check to see if the training you will receive is in the proper time frame. Ideally, being allowed to serve as an apprentice and sit in on your teacher's classes should be an integral part of your training.
4. Ask the length of your teacher training. Will it be an ongoing apprenticeship or will it be a weekend workshop? Will your training consist of a few hours, days, weeks, or years?
5. Check to see if there is any ongoing support after the training, or an opportunity to practice with others after the workshop. Also ask whether the teacher will be available for you after the workshop.
6. Ask whether you will receive a certificate at the completion of your teachers training.
7. Determine whether you feel the cost is reasonable and whether you will be supplied with a reference manual. Is the training value for money?
8. Ask if you are able to take notes in the class or record the information presented.
9. Does your teacher offer a formal application for your teacher training, including a statement of purpose and intention.
10. What support materials will be made available for you as part of your training? For example: written information, advice, details on the attunement procedures, symbols etc...
11. When will your Reiki teacher give you the final attunement, which bestows your ability to be a Reiki teacher in the lineage and how long before you will be able to initiate others and for which Reiki levels?
12. Ask whether your teacher has the experience to teach you to be a teacher.
13. Ask whether they have taught any Reiki teachers prior to you.

The first steps to becoming a Reiki teacher

Purpose and personal motivation

In making the decision to become a Reiki teacher, we must first examine our mind and our motivations as to whether we truly wish to step upon the teacher's path.

To illustrate why purpose is so important, imagine your life without it. Think of a journey you might take, a destination which you desire to reach. You may have your vehicle, but without your map *(purpose)* and your intention *(drive)* how will you achieve your goal? If driving blindly, with no clear direction of your destination, it would not be long before you are utterly lost and have no idea where you are going.

It is with purpose that we make clear decisions, putting our best foot forward and taking the necessary steps to complete our goal. The very act of setting a clear purpose can make every difference in our lives, whether this be as simple as *'what am I going to do today'*, to *'what am I going to do with the rest of my life'*. Often times neither will be clear, however, giving a positive and realistic intention to any given situation, will certainly see results.

The following questionnaire is designed to provide just that. This particular questionnaire is used as part of our teacher training programme and it is at this point that we sort out the serious candidate from the not so serious.

By addressing the following questions in an honest and truthful manner, it becomes apparent where our purpose, intention and true motivation lies.

If one is seriously considering the teacher's path, it is very worthwhile to consider ones' motives. What follows is the International Institute for Reiki Training's Teacher Training Personal Assessment Questionnaire. If you are interested, take a walk through this questionnaire, as it may assist you in gaining a clearer perspective of your personal motivation for becoming a teacher of Reiki and if you are already a teacher, it may serve to clarify or re-connect you to the higher goal of teaching Reiki.

Motivation has a great deal of importance in a teacher's path. The way that we approach teaching and our personal view of life, assists in determining how we are as a teacher and just as important, how we are in life.

Assessment and Questionnaire

The following questionnaire is a guide for self-evaluation, which we use at our Reiki Institute, both to evaluate the student's personal motivation and as a form of self-analysis. This is perhaps the most important factor.

If you are considering teacher training (or you are already a teacher), take the time to answer these questions for yourself.

Part A

1. In the past, what have I realised in the areas of...
   - Family
   - Work
   - Friendships
   - Relationships
   - Spiritual Path
   - My Shadow (our dark side)
   - Personal Growth
2. What have I wanted but never had in these areas?
3. What brings me out of harmony in relation to...
   A. My path?
   B. About myself?
4. What are my greatest fears in relation to...
   A. My path?
   B. About myself?
5. What roles do I play in my life? Which of these serve my path?
6. What do I need to do right now to further my journey along my path? How can I take action?
7. What are my strengths? What are my weaknesses?
8. What is my definition of myself as a teacher of Reiki?
9. What is my purpose in this life? How can I fulfil this purpose?

Part B

Essay approximately 1000 words.

Write as honestly and authentically as you know how (warts and all!).....

"Why do I want to be a Reiki teacher and what does this mean to me?"

Progressive Reiki training

Learning the Third Degree of Reiki varies from teacher to teacher. Some apprenticeships last many years, whereas some Reiki teachers will pass this level after only one day! The Third Degree in traditional Reiki circles, affords a more integrated and progressive form of learning.

Some Reiki teachers consider the Third Degree to be a single level, whilst other teachers break the Third Degree into two stages:

Stage one being the attunement for the third level, along with the methodologies and practices.

Stage two takes the form of a formal apprenticeship where the teacher in training participates and eventually assists the teacher in their own classes. Some schools have very stringent guidelines for accomplishing this level, whilst others simply allow the energy of Reiki to teach the prospective student.

The emphasis on becoming a teacher is to know that one is always a student. Every class and student brings new opportunities to learn. When we become a teacher we are a mirror to our students and a model for them to develop their own practice.

Although some Reiki teachers in training consider the Third Degree as a completion of the Reiki stages, it really is a new beginning. Reiki Mastery is a Mastery of one's self, an opening to a new beginning and new way of being.

Researching Reiki and knowing your subject

If you intend to become a teacher of Reiki, it is important to have an equal balance in knowledge and experience. Although I recommend a greater percentage of direct experience over knowledge, some knowledge is necessary because, the simple fact of the matter is that your students will ask you many questions. Rather than looking stupid, having an accurate answer will help your student's development and confidence in you as a guide on their spiritual journey.

One of the best ways to gain knowledge of Reiki is to read as many books as you can on the subject.

There have been some excellent guides to Reiki which have been written over the recent years and in addition to the information presented in *The Reiki Guide*, there are a wealth of great books on Reiki.*

---

* See our recommended reading list at the end of this book.

Although it can burn a hole in your hip pocket to purchase so many Reiki books, it is a good investment as a reference guide for your future as a teacher of Reiki. Alternatively, most public libraries now stock books on Reiki. Some of the first Reiki titles, published about 20 years ago are still the best.

The Internet is also an invaluable tool, as well as being a colossal wealth of information on the subject of Reiki. Just key 'Reiki' into any search engine and you will get literally millions of Reiki websites. This of course, can be a little daunting and one does need to skim through with a discerning mind. Just as there are excellent websites on Reiki, there are also many examples of the 'not so excellent'. The internet is also a great way to obtain specific information as well as networking and gaining helpful relationships with other Reiki practitioners and teachers world-wide.

Many Reiki websites contain a great deal of information, and although one should not under any circumstances copy the material of another, these already established structures can serve as a model for your own development and how you may wish to create your own unique view of Reiki.

Honouring your Reiki Lineage

As we further our journey to Mastery, it can be of great assistance to establish a firm resolve to contemplate your Reiki lineage and the founder, Mikao Usui. As with the attunements in our previous training, we become part of the Lineage. Here, in this important role as a teacher, we deepen that connection.

The following meditation can assist this connection, by strengthening our bonds to the lineage of Reiki.

Reiki Lineage Meditation

When we embark on the journey towards Mastery, it is a good idea to use the power of our intention as an invitation to all those forces that would assist us in our connection to this next phase in our Reiki development.

The following meditation is not a traditional Reiki meditation, however, it serves as a way to turn our mind towards the Reiki tradition and from whence it has sprung.

To do this meditation, you will need the names of your prospective Reiki lineage, beginning with the founder, Mikao Usui. If you do not know your teacher's Reiki lineage then ask them, as they should know it. If you cannot determine this, then just skip the second stage (teachers between Usui and yourself). The Meditation is as follows:

Imagine you are in a sacred hall and at the end of this hall are a series of doors. Each door has the name of each teacher in your Reiki lineage. Behind the first door stands Usui, behind the second door is the next teacher in your Reiki lineage. Behind the third door is the next teacher in your Reiki lineage, and so on. The second last door is your Reiki teacher and the final door is a mirrored reflection of your self as a teacher.

As you approach the first door, you see the words 'Mikao Usui' written as a plaque on the door. You go up to the door and it opens. You enter the room and see Mikao Usui standing there. In the room is a gift for Mikao Usui and this may be a material or symbolic gift, or something that you say to honour Mikao Usui and his tradition.

Bestow this gift to the Sensei. In return, Mikao Usui has something for you. This time, he presents you with a gift. Allow whatever you imagine to flow out of the meditation. This may be an object, an attunement, an acknowledgement, a teaching, or a single word.

Once you have received this gift give thanks to Mikao Usui and make the promise to honour his tradition.

You now leave the room and the door closes behind you. Here, once again, you are facing the hall of doors. You now proceed to the next door and standing behind this door the next teacher in your Reiki lineage appears. Follow the same steps as before, offering a gift to the Sensei and receiving one in return, finally stating your vow to them and learning.

Then proceed with each successive door. This process is repeated until you reach your own teacher. You give your gift; receive a gift in return and make the strong promise to uphold the Reiki tradition.

Finally, you come to the last door. Here behind this door is yourself, but not you as you are now, but your future self, as a teacher. Go inside, greet your future self and give yourself a gift.

In return, your future self gives you a gift and you make the strong promise to yourself to uphold the Reiki tradition. Once you have completed this process, review your gifts, both given and received. When you feel ready, bring your awareness back to the present.

This ends the meditation.

This mediation serves as a way to acknowledge your connection to your Reiki lineage and the act of imagined gifts serves to generate a positive aspiration and act of generosity. It is suggested to use this meditation on a regular basis throughout your teacher training. It is also a beneficial mediation for established teachers as well.

The responsibilities of becoming a Reiki teacher

What many people do not realise when stepping upon the teachers' path is that one steps into a great responsibility. This is understood in two stages:

The first is a responsibility to oneself. As a teacher of Reiki, it is your responsibility to be a living example of Reiki and its practice in the world. One cannot be an effective teacher and embody this without a deep personal commitment to upholding the tradition, maintaining the integrity of personal practice, as well as attending to your personal development and effectively 'living Reiki'.

The second responsibility is the way we shape the lives of the students we teach. This is not to say that we are responsible for our students' actions. If I was responsible for all my students' actions, I don't know where I'd be, but seriously, this kind of responsibility comes in the form of doing ones best to pass on the Reiki tradition, making sure our students have understood what has been taught and, where possible, being available for our students in a supportive role.

Leadership and teaching Reiki

In becoming a teacher of Reiki, one is better served by being aware of certain leadership qualities. A student will hardly put their trust in you as a teacher if you cannot lead your class with some certainty.

In Buddhism this is illustrated in three ways:

> The first is to lead as a King, ruling over one's subjects and protecting the Kingdom.
> The second is to be like a Boatman. Here, everyone crosses the river together as one, to reach the shore.
> The third is that of a Shepherd. The Shepherd puts their herd before them, so it is that to be a Shepherd is to serve, for the benefit of others.

Leadership can be facilitated by any of these three means, but the ideal is to be as a Shepherd, acting in such a way to benefit as many as possible and not just to gain notoriety or fame for oneself.

The 10 keys to leadership for Reiki Teachers

Below are ten points which can be applied to being a leader in Reiki*:

1. **Self-knowledge.** For one to be a leader, one needs to know the material one is teaching. If one is blundering through the material and constantly having to refer to one's notes, no intelligent student will maintain their trust in a teacher like this, for long. Self knowledge is paramount to leading a class with conviction.

2. **Fairness.** One must be fair and just in their actions. Without demonstrating fair and just actions, a student will not be inspired to maintain respect for a teacher. Respect cannot be commanded, it comes by embodying virtue and by living your dharma. It is not enough to have ideas of what it means to embody this; we need to be actively involved with it, on a daily basis.

3. **Confidence and Presence.** A teacher should possess confidence and presence. These qualities are cultivated with time and experience; however a new teacher can emulate these qualities with sincerity, by adopting a confident attitude. From this state of mind comes presence and over time, one can genuinely build these qualities more and more.

4. **Humility.** A teacher must demonstrate humility and never assume superiority over another. A teacher who demonstrates equality and is still prepared to do the work he would ask of a student, demonstrates an ability to be on par with others. The teacher should be vulnerable, equal, and compassionate in his actions. A teacher needs to lead by example, but beyond this, be willing to do more than is expected of their own students.

5. **Living example**. Few students can learn, unless by example. *'Do as I say, not as I do'*. This attitude will not endure respect from a student, nor will it serve to instil faith in the teacher, if they are not prepared to get down and get their hands dirty once in a while. One must 'walk the talk'.

6. **Co-operation.** A teacher should encourage co-operation, as many parts make a whole. If a teacher can organise and delegate where needed, as well as assist one's students to work in a co-operative manner, this will encourage a sense of oneness, equality and

---

* This is an adaptation from Think and Grow Rich, by Napoleon Hill (Wilshire Book Company, 1966)

camaraderie within the group. The result is a harmonious balance of energies.

7. **Maintaining right views of competitors.** If a teacher outwardly condemns their competition, they may come across as being arrogant or exclusive. Whereas, if one expresses a universal approach to the bigger picture, that all beings are on their journey and that what is right for one, may not be the same for another, then the teacher will be viewed as being fair. If one takes this approach, others will follow.

8. **Honest communication.** How one communicates and what one says is very important. Gossip, spreading rumours and speculation about others soon turns into gospel and what goes around will come back at you twice as hard.

   One should never be seen to gossip and one should discourage gossip when possible. Being honest and open in communication is a principle to uphold and it begins with the teacher.

9. **Relinquishing title.** One should downplay titles which put a teacher upon a pedestal. Where possible, one should also remove the pedestals placed under one's feet by students. Regardless of one's spiritual ability, egotism has no place in Reiki, or any spiritual tradition. Respect, as both teacher and leader comes from exemplifying one's moral and ethical example. If one needs to inflate their ego to summon respect and loyalty from their students, the effect will be transparent and the teacher will fall. A Master of Reiki does not need to tell everyone their Master status, a master is recognised by their merits and by being a living example. By this alone is a Master true to the teachings.

10. **Praise and Validation.** For a new student, appropriate encouragement is very important. Offering thanks for your students time and willingness to learn and encouraging your students' development is extremely helpful in creating a supportive teacher/student relationship. Once this relationship and trust is present, more precise and direct means of awakening can effectively be transmitted.

16
Mentorship

The Teacher/Student Relationship
What draws a student to a teacher is what the teacher can offer the student. The student will check out what the teacher has to offer and is often motivated by three factors.

These being:

- **Money.** How much will the training cost me?
- **Convenience.** How far will I need to travel to get to the course?
- **Time.** How much time will I need to invest to reach a desired outcome?

These are indeed worth consideration and it is important to use ones common sense when making the decision to learn. On a deeper level, a student is drawn to a teacher due to sympathetic resonance. When two vibrations are in accord with each other, they flow together. A student is drawn to a teacher not only for practical reasons, but due to sympathetic resonance. It is our own vibration, meeting in accord with theirs.

We have all had this experience in our lives. When we meet someone for the first time one of three things happen:

1. We feel a strong attraction and in no time at all we instantly feel like old friends.
2. We feel a strong aversion and immediately feel uncomfortable in their presence.
3. We feel neutral.

When we experience the first or second response, it is an indication that we have a karmic connection to the person. The reason I include the secondary experience (even though the experience is perceived as negative), it nonetheless is the result of previous karma. The person who triggers disturbing emotions has much to teach us about ourselves. We can consider someone who we feel a strong aversion to as a great teacher in our personal and spiritual development.

The 3 stages of the Teacher/Student Relationship

A teacher should understand the stages that progress between the teacher and the student. As the relationship develops, these roles change. The following are three common stages:

Stage 1 Teacher/Student – The Childhood stage
In this stage, the student sees the teacher as a model of how he or she will be as a healer. A student models themself on the teacher's methods, actions and approach to healing. At this stage the student has some ideals of their own, but fails to have the conviction to be strong in their own view. They look up to the teacher like a parent figure and look to them for guidance.

Stage 2 Teacher/Student – Adolescent stage
At this point in the relationship, the student sees themself as having accomplished a sound understanding of the material and desire to be acknowledged by their teacher for this level of understanding. Usually at this stage, a student begins to form personal ideas regarding their personal style and may question the teacher's position, ability, ethical behaviour and approach. This is quite normal and an essential stage for the student in developing their own uniqueness as a practitioner of the Reiki system.

Stage 3 Teacher/Teacher – Adulthood stage
Here, the teacher, or practitioner-in-training has formed a clear understanding of the Reiki system and has found their place as a teacher or practitioner in their own right. It is at this stage that the relationship has completely evolved to where the teacher in training, or practitioner is almost on a par with their teacher. There is an equal respect and acknowledgement of separate and common views and a mutual respect for one another.

Mentorship and apprenticing

Mentorship is an essential part of being a teacher. One's ability to mentor a student through their journey in Reiki and to nurture their progress during the various levels, aids in a student's development within the Reiki system. Being a mentor is to be a friend on the path and a guide for another. Being a mentor does not necessarily stop with being able to answer the student's questions, it goes further by offering advice and being available to support and guide the student with personal issues as well as the development of their healing abilities.

Serving an apprenticeship becomes more of a focus when a student makes a decision to become a teacher. Although the actual methodology of the initiation procedures takes only a few days to grasp, it is the inner practice which is fostered during a practitioner's teacher training, that makes a formal apprenticeship an essential part of learning.

The length of Reiki teacher training

An apprenticeship may take anywhere from six months to several years and involves ongoing practice and commitment to attending Reiki classes, as well as participating in clinical sessions and private consultations. One can only gain an understanding of this process through practice and the application of these methods in a class environment.

Many Reiki teachers now offer teacher training in two stages. Reiki 3A being an introduction to the methods of the Level 3 symbol, its applications, the method of initiation or attunement procedures and so forth. In the 3A stage, students are exposed to the teachers' level of Reiki energy and it is usually from this point that one gains insight into whether this is really a path one wishes to continue. Once a student is sure of their path to teach Reiki, the 3B stage, or apprenticeship, can begin.

Although some Reiki teachers do not offer extensive training to becoming a teacher, this is perhaps the most important role any Reiki teacher can offer. It is great to teach Reiki to people, but it is better to teach another how to be a teacher. The field of merit is far wider and the benefit to humanity can grow as you cast your net wide by instructing another how to pass the Reiki teachings on to others, who can in turn offer the same.

17
Pre-attunement guidelines

Preparation prior to giving Reiki attunements
The following are some preliminaries before we embark upon the path of Reiki initiation.

Before we begin the process of initiation it is important to consider: our mental state; our environment; our emotions and our intention. Let us look at each of these points in more detail.

Our Mental State
Ideally, before we begin a Reiki class, we should where possible, find time to centre our awareness or meditate. A good way to facilitate this is to make sure you set up for the workshop the evening before or if this is not possible, then to get an early start. One of the quickest ways to lose your centre before a class, is to be still setting up the room as people are arriving. You then have to deal with last minute set up requirements and student registrations. This will leave you no real time to mentally prepare yourself.

The golden rule is to allow yourself plenty of time in the morning before the class starts. If your location and time permits, a short time in nature is of great benefit in aligning your bodies' energy. Even if this is finding a park in a busy city or some place in a natural setting, time spent in nature will enhance the bodies' energy and clarify your mind.

Another way to assist in settling your mind is to have some of your previous students assist you with setting up the space, as well as taking the registrations prior to the seminar commencing, so you have the mental space to prepare for giving the Reiki attunements and reviewing what you will teach.

Our Environment

It is important to choose the right space for teaching Reiki. It is necessary to have a clean, well ordered and sound space for conducting a Reiki class. Certainly, the physical appearance of the room should be pleasing to the eye. When we set up a room, we should consider the space much like a mandala. The way we arrange all the parts with good intention and purpose affect the whole energy of a room.

Making an extra effort to pay attention to finer details like the balance and arrangement of furniture; the symmetry of objects in the room and the like, will add balance and presence to the room. Other suggestions might be the setting of a simple shrine, lighting a candle, some incense, *(make sure you use only high quality incense and not too much),* aromatherapy, *(provided you know how to blend and vaporise oils)* and arranging some flowers adds a nice touch to the class room.

It is not necessary to make this an entire production, but simple touches to a room assist in promoting harmonious energies. Having some soothing music in the background also assists in creating a gentle mood, so choose your music with care.

Our Emotional state and intention

Where we are within our emotions also plays an important role in teaching. The first place to start is to identify where we are in terms of our moods and emotions. The ideal time to do this is when we are giving ourselves quiet time before the class begins. Once we have identified our emotional state whether this is perceived as good, bad, or neutral, we can then cultivate a positive and aware state.

A good way to start, is to place your hands on your heart centre and generate a smile. The very act of smiling generates positive energy for the whole body. We smile inwardly, like we are smiling in our hearts. It is at this point we may do a number of things. Some suggestions are to visualise the workshop flowing with ease. We imagine that we are seeing all the participants open, happy and content with their results. You can also imagine yourself teaching the class, being articulate and enjoying the experience of passing on the Reiki attunements.

Another option is to do affirmations in your mind, stating that: *"I am a clear vessel for Universal healing energy. Divine energy fills my body. Divine energy fills my speech. Divine energy fills my mind. All that I am, do and say is an emanation of pure Divine energy"* or words to this effect.

Another excellent preparation is to give oneself a Reiki self-attunement procedure. This is a direct way of summoning a vast amount of healing energy to yourself and to experience healing on many levels.

18

Reiki Attunements and tips for teachers

Learning the Reiki Attunements – How to approach it

It goes without saying that in order to be effective whilst facilitating the Reiki initiations, one needs practice. This is where self-attunement procedures are very important, especially maintaining a consistency with all initiation procedures and making sure each initiation is not only performed correctly in sequence, but that each symbol is carefully and consciously drawn. It's all too easy for the mind to get lazy whilst performing initiation procedures, so correct concentration plays a big part.

Beyond the mechanics of the initiation procedures, comes the intuitive flow which is gained through years of practice and daily application. We may experience fleeting moments of this during the procedures, which is quite normal, considering we are placing our awareness in a non-ordinary state of consciousness.

With time and personal practice of the initiation procedures, the experience of this universal flow becomes more and more stable within our being. The initiation then requires no thought, no effort, as the physical mind is free of inner dialogue, no longer wandering about. The only sound is that of the symbols mantra, the only image is that of the symbols form and one is in complete union with the energy. Total focus and concentration are present with absolute clarity.

Not everyone will experience this heightened state of awareness all of the time during initiations, but with on-going development, this spontaneous state will arise more often.

The Reiki attunements in detail

A teacher of Reiki should not only know how to give a sound Reiki attunement, they should also know some different ways. Here, we will give recommendations on how to get the most out of attunements for oneself and others.

When we closely examine the Reiki attunements, we find one common thread and that is that they vary greatly from one Reiki lineage to the next.

As part of my own personal exploration of various Reiki systems, having been privy to numerous Reiki manuals and attunement processes, the elements of symbol, mythology, and sequence are completely prevalent throughout the Reiki world.

It seems that almost everyone has their own personal style of Reiki attunement and for the most part, most attunement procedures work, *(though some are more effective than others)*. Ultimately, one needs to look at the results. If, at the end of the attunement, the individual has a strong, yet gentle source of unlimited healing energy emanating from their palms which has a lasting effect, then regardless of the method used, the main thing is that it worked!

So, what if this has not been your experience? My answer would be to contact your teacher and examine what they know. Because the transference of Reiki energy is dependant upon a carrier of this energy, much like a large family tree, one requires their parent, in this case their Reiki teacher, to have the necessary transmission.

It goes without saying that for one to have a sound connection to Reiki energy, your teacher is of the upmost importance. You need your teacher for guidance and you need your teacher for the transmissions. But you need a good teacher if you are going to make real progress.

Staying grounded during Reiki attunements

A common result of facilitating Reiki attunements is a feeling of ungroundedness or feeling 'spacey'. As we are being a conduit for the Reiki energy, this high resonant energy tends to make the mind and bodies boundaries fluid. As a result, we 'space out', or feel light headed and may experience a variety of sensations, which is perfectly understandable when we consider the practices and interaction we are having with the Universal energy.

The question is: How do we keep our feet on the ground?

The following methods are helpful in maintaining a grounded space when giving attunements or Reiki treatments in general.

1. Eat more. Although you may feel inclined to eat lightly when performing attunements, intentionally eat more heavy or bulk foods. Eating meat (if you're so inclined), grains and vegetables which are grown in or on the ground will pull your energies down and keep yourself focussed. These yang energies assist the bodies' energy to be earthed.

2. Curl your toes. Curling your toes directs awareness to your feet. This method can be done during healing work or even during initiations, to assist in maintaining a grounded space. You simply curl your toes as if you are trying to pick up an object with your toes.

3. Hara breathing. Direct your breath deep into your navel. You may even imagine your breath is going down to your feet.

4. Visualization techniques. There are also a variety of visualizations that can be applied. Here are just a few:

   A. Visualize your feet are the roots of a tree which anchor you to the earth's core, or that your feet extend beyond your physical body and lie deep in the earth.

   B. Visualize the power symbol from the Second Degree and imagine this symbol spiralling down through your legs and into the earth.

   C. Imagine you are wearing boots made of lead or that your feet are made from lead and hold you heavy to the ground.

5. Your environment. If you are in a hot environment, wear lighter clothes, if your body is too hot, it is easy to associate this with sleep. Having fresh air and a well ventilated room will keep your mind sharp and assist in maintaining a grounded state of consciousness.

6. Physical Activity. Having regular exercise will also assist you in grounding your body. Whether this is a walk at the beach or in nature, gardening or physical exercise, like running, swimming, or working out, digging trenches or chopping wood, it's up to you. Be sure not to overdo it and seek advice as to what is the best kind of exercise for you, from fitness professionals.

7. Sex. As well as being an excellent and most enjoyable form of exercise, the act of love making directly grounds the bodies' energies. Sex will not only improve one's mood, but give the body balance of male and female energies, as well as grounding on the physical level.

19

A Reiki teacher's development

The Teacher's appearance and cultivating presence

Whilst teaching Reiki, it is worth considering your outward appearance. One should always be well groomed and present oneself in a manner which will be pleasing to others. When you are teaching Reiki to a new group of students, they will often spend the first few hours 'sizing you up' and so very often people judge a book by its cover. You can assist the student with this outer projection by presenting yourself in a neat and organized way. This also is a reflection on your inner state of mind.

If you are outwardly messy, what does this say about your inner awareness? The outer should match the inner and the inner should match the outer. Take a moment to consider this in relation to your own life and see what areas of your inner or outer landscape may require attention.

On the subject of generating presence, you need to create a space where your students will instantly feel calm in your presence. Here, the preparation starts before the class. Ideally, you may wish to have an assistant help you with setting up the space, as well as attending to the minor details before you teach.

If you have ever been in the presence of a truly accomplished master, whether this be of Reiki or Meditation or some other spiritual practice, you will immediately feel a presence about them. This 'power field' as it is often described, is the Masters' accumulated blessing and one feels a deep trust and joy, just being close to a being like this.

The thing is, we can't just expect to embody this level of presence immediately, as it takes many dedicated years of practice to embody this level of accomplishment. However, we can do our best to be friendly, joyful and sincere when greeting our students. I have observed that some new teachers can become overly stiff or fixed and take themselves far too seriously. Then there are those who become very holy. The bad thing about too much spiritual pride is that you are always in poor company because no one is on your level.

Dealing with personal issues

At times during our teaching life, we will find that life continues to bring up our personal issues. When we have problems in our own lives, it makes teaching others a genuine struggle. If you find yourself in a personal crisis, then it is important to acknowledge this and seek guidance from a trusted therapist.

If one is teaching and life is full of distraction and conflict, then one should deal with such issues, rather than bring this disrupted energy into the class. Energy is felt by others and although you may be good at putting on a brave face, your students will pick up with an intuitive feeling that something is out of order and this is definitely something to avoid.

So, it is important that one has one's life in order to teach Reiki properly. Often we participate in life's big dramas and we become entangled, thinking that it is in our best interest to take the lead role. When stepping upon the path of teaching, many obstacles and personal problems arise. If we can create a supportive space around us we will have a better chance of finding resolve during these difficult times. If you feel you need to take a break from teaching or treating others, take the time.

Most important of all, be yourself. Be natural and show an active interest in your students' lives. A person will have a natural affinity with you, if you start by taking an active interest in them. Remember your students' names, lavish compliments on them, but do so with sincerity. By following these guidelines, you will be well on the way to establishing presence, which will hold you in good stead for building positive relationships in the future.

Effective listening and being open

When we begin teaching others Reiki or even when administering a treatment, listening to the student or client is most important. In the case of treating others, the initial interview can be a wealth of information regarding the clients' needs and how you may assist with their healing. Be sure to listen to what they have to say, ask questions about their problem and observe everything about them. Body language is an excellent source of information. Notice their physical appearance, how they speak and how they hold their hands. Do they lean forward or distance themselves? It takes time to generate a skill in reading people however, if you can fine tune this ability it will assist you in determining the best course of action for the individual's healing process. Neuro Linguistic Programming or N.L.P., offers many tried and tested methods in understanding the language of the body, so if this interests you, read up on the subject or take a short course. You will find it most useful.

When teaching others, encourage the participants to share experiences. Maintain eye contact with your students, invite questions, and be supportive when comments are made. For example: *"That is an important question, thankyou for asking that"*, or *"Jane's experiences demonstrate this point clearly…"* involve your students in the learning process and encourage an open forum for discussion. Your students should be encouraged to think and question what is being taught. I often say in my own classes not to take anything I have said for granted, but to experience these things for yourself.

Your students will also teach you much about yourself, if you are willing to listen and learn from them. We are all mirrors of each other and very often, what we experience will trigger a response in another. Also, remind your students to ask questions and create time for exploration. It is important to mention that there is no such thing as a dumb question and that if a student has a question, more than likely others will have the same question in their minds as well. Much can be learnt in this way, because what is required will come forth.

Part of effective listening is to be fully aware of the dialogue taking place. Once you have formulated your response and you are clear on what you would like to say, share from your heart space and be concise.

Communicating in this way is a time honoured tradition amongst traditional indigenous societies, where silence was used to create space for contemplation and clear dialogue.

Other helpful ways of listening involve matching body language. Here, we mirror the student's body language. If they have their hands on their lap, place your hands on your lap and so on. Many times when we are involved with someone, we do this subconsciously. Take advantage of this useful advice and you can then learn to listen and come to know your students from a more intimate level.

Setting personal boundaries

Whether we are facilitating an attunement procedure or giving a Reiki session, attending to our personal boundaries is always important. So often we begin healing work, without the awareness of our personal energetic space and that of our client.

The following methods are various ways of establishing and maintaining personal boundaries during healing work.

Method #1 Sealing the Thymus Chakra

This method uses the 'harmony' symbol from Second Degree Reiki to establish a high resonance energy field over the gland governing our immune system. The thymus Chakra is situated in the upper chest and is at the point where our collar bones meet. This is an area where we are prone to transference of lower energy. By placing a high resonance energy field over this area *(in the form of a Reiki symbol)*, we effectively create a protective boundary, thereby creating a field which is no longer prone to transference of lesser energies.

The method is as follows: Place one hand over your thymus Chakra (upper chest) and the other hand on the back of the thymus Chakra, where the neck and shoulders meet.

Visualize the symbol beneath your hands in the colour blue. You may wish to use a Reiki symbol in this case, or simply energise this point with Reiki energy. If you are using a Reiki symbol for this exercise, state the name (mantra) of the symbol three times and visualise drawing it beneath your palms.

The use of three mantra repetitions, affirms a strong impression on the subconscious. This establishes your personal boundaries throughout the healing procedure. A further extension of this technique is to imagine that one has a blue bubble or sphere of light around oneself. This represents a force field which transmutes any lesser energies as soon as they contact it.

Method #2 Deity Invocation

If you are familiar with specific archetypes in the Tibetan Buddhist tradition, you may wish to use a Buddha form as a point of focus. One may evoke a deity to reside above one's head during a Reiki treatment or whilst facilitating an initiation procedure.

The specific deity used is best determined by your familiarity with the deity.

If for example, the deity is the Buddha of compassion, one would visualize this form, either above one's head or residing in one's heart. The practitioner then requests this archetype's blessing and protection throughout the procedure. If a particular mantra is connected with the visualization, one repeats this silently in one's mind. For the above example, in the case of the Buddha of Compassion (Loving eyes) or Chenrezig [Tib.] one uses the mantra: OM MANI PAD ME HUNG.

Loving Eyes
(Tib. Chenrezig)

The mantra holds the awareness on the activity of the Buddha and energises the speech centre of the practitioner when repeated. This energy then maintains its presence throughout the session.

Once the session is complete, it is also important to put things away. When a particular archetype is evoked, this presence should be put away or dissolved back into space.

Alternatively, one may also use archetypes from other spiritual or religious traditions such as: Jesus, Krishna, Angels, a Guide, a Totem, or some other archetype which has meaning for you.

Method #3 Psychic Armour

In this method we visualise and contain our personal power using armour in a visualized process. We first generate a positive feeling in our body, generating good will and compassion for all that lives. We then imagine that solid armour forms over our bodies, covering all areas with impenetrable strength. Similarly, we may avert negative energies by imagining flames emanating from our bodies in all directions, to dispel any negative energy. Visualizing fire may seem quite forceful to some however, these aspects of the visualization are used to remove harmful energies from oneself. Therefore, the intention is that any unwanted energies are purified by the flames of positive activity.

For less disruptive energies, one may visualize more gentle symbols, such as white light, or a crystal sphere of positive energy shining out in all directions, transmuting and averting any negative energy.

20
Spiritual development

The Secret to Spiritual Strength
In general, maintaining good personal boundaries comes from ongoing spiritual practice, daily purification practices and cultivating a positive mind. The reason for this is, one naturally maintains good personal boundaries through ongoing cultivation of positive impressions, as well as having a good outlook on life.

If you are full of positive energy, no lesser energy can affect you. Like switching on a light in a darkened room, instantly the darkness is dispelled. It is the same with cultivating a positive mind. By dedicating wellness and happiness to all beings, one strengthens one's personal protection. You should also pay attention to the bodies needs in terms of adequate rest, exercise and maintaining a positive attitude towards life. Spending more time with like minded individuals and seeking the necessary amount of time for relaxation, play and reconnection will naturally aid the body and mind.

Connecting with nature will also bring the mind and the bodies' energies into balance. Spending time in an old forest; walking in nature; hiking; swimming in natural streams or in the ocean, all aid in bringing the body and mind into a balanced state. For most of us, we live in cities, so nature is often far removed from our daily lives. It is vitally important to connect with nature and a natural environment on a regular basis, for this not only brings health to our body and mind, it also brings deep peace.

Lastly, meditate daily, if only for five minutes, as this will strengthen your mind. Take this piece of advice as if it were the only medicine you need to cure the disease of ignorance.

Cultivating your spiritual self

When we speak of our relationship with self, the "I' or the "me", it can often be confusing as to where the spiritual self resides, in the bigger picture. In truth, to view the spiritual self one need not make a separation between ordinary life and spiritual life, for they run parallel. The problem is that many people make distinction between spiritual practice and their "ordinary lives". For example, *"Right now I'm being spiritual"*, and, *"I'm now attending to the house work"*, or *"I'm now paying the bills"*, or *"Now I'm spending time being a parent"*, or *"Now I'm spending time with my spouse"*. All of these distinctions are separations between one aspect of 'self' and another. Why not integrate the spiritual with the mundane? To be in balance with the universe, mindfulness and awareness is the key. One can be spiritual and do the house work. Is not the house work a spiritual practice of itself? There is no need to make a separation between our meditation practice and our life as meditation. Just as you get up from your meditation cushion, a new meditation begins.

By resting in awareness, knowing that every sound is perfect speech and every thought is wisdom, that everyone is a Buddha, (they just may not see it yet) is a way to move through your day in a state of joy. When we have disturbing emotions arise, or disruptive thoughts that may judge ourself or others, recognise that this is a part of your mind which is simply playing out old dramas. Old dramas, after a while, become so embarrassingly out of fashion, that you just can't wear these trips in public anymore.

Think of these old impressions as nothing more than the impermanent comings and goings of the mind. They rise and fall. If we give them little energy, they will simply fall away and we can give rise to cultivating greater awareness, love and compassion for ourselves and those around us.

The more we can catch ourselves playing out the old movie and replace this with the new and more liberated one, the more we free ourselves to see what is really there. This is the free and unhindered, joyful expression of our minds. This frees up tremendous amounts of energy, as we no longer have to waste so much time and energy maintaining trips and dramas which serve no one, least of all ourselves.

Seeing the world as it really is, full of potential, meaning and wisdom, enables us to be truly useful, as we are no longer adding to problems around us. Instead, we are making space to benefit others.

When we do this, we can be an inspiration to others, an example and expression of Universal energy, which is boundless, alive and free. The thing is it's up to you. No one will do it for you. When you realise that you are the one who put yourself on the very cactus you are sitting on, you can take responsibility, get up, heal your backside and walk on, knowing that you have the choice to subdue your ignorance and walk on as a shining light for others to see.

Reiki and Spiritual development

The system of Reiki and especially teaching Reiki, amplifies one's spiritual evolution. When we consider that being a channel of Reiki purifies our own defilements in body, speech and mind, then giving Reiki empowerments expands the potential for spiritual development at a higher rate. As one of my teachers always says, *"If you have a lot of crap (personal problems and wrong views) you can make a lot of fertilizer"*. Disturbing emotions and wrong views are actually raw materials which can be transformed into the highest joy and wisdom when we purify our minds. Because we are working with the Reiki energy, a great many of these problems can present themselves on the path. Like the analogy of the mud at the bottom of the pond rising to the surface, the more we work with Reiki, the more opportunities present to discard old habits which no longer serve us. It is not uncommon to experience a number of ups and downs on our Reiki path. For teachers and especially at the beginning of one's teaching career, this can seem like a real roller coaster ride, but at least this is an indication that something good is actually happening.

One could become quite concerned if life simply became a steady stream, with nothing but harmony all of the time. Becoming a fit vessel for holding the Reiki lineage and associated responsibilities has its challenges, though these are usually about ourselves getting in the way of our own process. We need to purify these problems before a steady stream appears. Even then, a few snags will appear but with practice we learn to negotiate these without too many problems and can carry on with our journey.

When we give up the need to control the outcome of how we wish the spirit of Reiki to move in our lives, the more flow we create. When we are not hellbent on swimming upstream, rather, going with the flow, we can be gently carried to where we need to be and with whom. Teaching Reiki, much like the practice of hands-on healing, is a process of letting go. When we still our minds, keep our big mouths shut and be in the essence of healing energy, we become true conduits for the life force energy. Ultimately, this filters into our daily lives and just like rain washing away dust and debris from an obscured lens, we have a clear surface through which to view our world.

Learning from other teachers

There's a lot to be said for sitting in on other Reiki teachers' workshops. During my teacher training, I had the opportunity to attend a variety of Reiki workshops with various teachers. I learnt many new methods to add to my toolbox and learnt new ways to facilitate classes. I might add that I also learnt some new ways of how not to teach and what not to do. Reviewing previous levels with your Reiki teacher and learning from others, all adds to one's experience and development as a teacher.

The moral of the story is to never stop learning. Each time I attend workshops, I learn something new, even if it is only one thing. Simply being in the Reiki energy offers something every time. If you are keen on this idea, ask your teacher if they could recommend other teachers they know. Participating in other Reiki Teachers' workshops, *(even from different Reiki styles or lineages)* will broaden your view.

Co-teaching and class participation

Where possible, you should ask your Reiki instructor if you can sit in on their Reiki workshops. This is by far the best way to generate a good foundation, if you are to be a teacher yourself one day.

When I began my teacher training in Reiki, my first initiating masters didn't formally apprentice new teachers. I considered this of the upmost importance, plus I really enjoyed reviewing Reiki workshops. So I made myself available whenever possible to re-sit Reiki levels and to assist my teachers as much as I could. This began my informal apprenticeship and I learnt a great deal. As my motivation and dedication became apparent, my teachers gave me opportunities to teach or demonstrate some of the techniques and I gradually began to step into the role of an assisting teacher.

I found this process to be a valuable step towards cultivating the Reiki teacher within, and each seminar presented new lessons and a deeper understanding of the principles of Reiki.

Sadly, many new teachers in training seldom have the opportunity to learn in this way. The trend of 'churn them out' Reiki Master intensives, leaves no time for this important mentoring process and as a result, many teachers who learn this way seldom integrate the teachings in a stable and wholesome way. Much can be gained through formal apprenticeship and the support that comes with this, aids in the personal and spiritual growth that the Reiki system brings.

Support groups and Reiki Share

As part of your ongoing commitment to your students and their development, you may wish to offer support groups or monthly get-togethers. Some support groups are designed to give an open and supportive forum for students to share their experiences and ask questions regarding their practice. These groups are also an opportunity to practice the methods taught at the particular Reiki level. You may wish to create a beginners and advanced practitioners support group. Likewise, if your timetable does not permit this much time to offer such groups, it is a common practice to invite previous students to review a Reiki level at no or minimal cost. Reviewing a Reiki level is always a good idea. As a student, you will frequently gain new insights and gain a deeper understanding of the Reiki energy and related applications. By simply being in the Reiki energy, one benefits in the collective Reiki energy field generated

Whatever you decide to offer to students as a means of support and development, remember that it is up to the student to ultimately become self-reliant, and independent.

Healing clinics and community service

Another excellent forum for giving Reiki is through various community groups and health care organizations. Today, many hospitals are becoming more and more open to Reiki practitioners assisting patients in a complementary way, alongside conventional treatment. Working with Cancer patients, AIDS sufferers and in Hospice all can be rewarding and beneficial ways to put your Reiki skills into action.

Participating in these areas though, requires that a practitioner has good personal boundaries or as some say, 'a thick skin'. If you are an overly sensitive person, then perhaps this is an area which is not for you. When working with the terminally ill, one should attend to personal boundaries and have the necessary time off between treatments.

Community service is also an inspiration to others. When we look at greatly compassionate beings like Mother Teresa and the Dalai Lama, we see compassion in action. Through service to others, we can greatly assist our own journey and spiritual development. It is often said that service is the quick path.

21
The Path of Purification

Integration of Reiki Mastery – the path of Purification

Taking initiation into the Third Degree is not only a huge step in one's life as a healer, it also awakens our spiritual selves to the Reiki energy in a new way. Here, we change our relationship to the energy. To illustrate this relationship, we can use the analogy of a 'water well'. The well is owned by a kind lord, who allows the water carrier to take water from the pure crystal spring and carry it to each home in the neighbourhood. Here, the water carrier is the initiated teacher of Reiki, who dispenses the water *(Reiki energy)* to the homes in the neighbourhood *(students)*. The kind lord is Medicine Buddha *(an enlightened state of wellness)*, and the spring is the Universal Healing Energy.

Medicine Buddha
(Tib. Sangye Menlha)

What this example illustrates is the relationship of a teacher of Reiki. The mind of Reiki is Medicine Buddha and the spring is the Universal Energy. The water carrier's bucket is our body and the role of being a water carrier is the bestowal of the attunements to others.

The essence of Reiki is to generate a strong bond with the spring, or energy and to have a sound and clean bucket to carry the water to others.

In other words, we should become fit vessels for the Universal energy. Through ongoing practice, we purify ourselves in body, in our speech and in our minds. In doing this, our vessels to carry the energy become clean, clear and thereby honour the purity of what we give to others. In the same way that we would not serve a fine vintage red wine out of a dirty plastic cup, so it is with our body.

So how do we nurture this process of purification, so that we might become the vessel we aspire to be?

The following are some methods we can use to align ourselves with the Reiki energy and purify our Reiki channel.

Techniques for Purification
In the Usui Reiki Ryoho tradition *(Japanese Reiki style)* we find two very useful techniques for purifying the body. The first of these techniques comes from the founder, Mikao Usui and is a traditional method for removing unwanted lower energy from the body. The second technique comes from Hiroshi Doi, a member of the Reiki Gakkai *(Japanese Reiki learning society)* and is one of his practices for purification.

Kenyoku-ho – The traditional method of dry bathing
This is a technique which helps to cleanse and enhance your energy field while disconnecting yourself from outside influences. A literal translation of Kenyoku is 'dry bath'. Ken means drought; dry; drink up; heaven; emperor'; Yoku means: 'bathe; be favoured with; bask in', and ho means 'technique; method or way'. This is an original technique from Mikao Usui.

The Technique:
1. Sit or stand comfortably.
2. Place your hands in prayer position, hands folded at heart level, with your fingers pointing away from your body at a slight angle. Calm your mind and say silently: *"I begin Kenyoku-ho now"*.

3. Place your right hand's fingertips near the top of your left shoulder *(where the collarbone and shoulder meet)*. Hand is flat, palm toward body.

4. Take in a breath before each sweep, as this assists in releasing excess energy from your energy field.

5. In one motion, move your hand downward in a diagonal line, from the left shoulder to the right hip and flick off. Imagine your hand is a magnet for all negative and congested energies and that these are collected in your palm. As you flick off these energies, they are transformed into positive energy.

6. Repeat movements with the left hand, on the right side of the body in the same way. Moving your left hand in a downward diagonal line, from the right shoulder to the left hip.

7. Repeat this once again on the left shoulder. *(Twice on left hand side*

and once on right hand side).

8. Now place your right hand on the left upper arm or shoulder, palm facing down, hand flat, fingers pointing outwards. In one motion, move the right hand down the arm, to the finger tips and flick off *(shake hand to release excess energy).*
9. Repeat this motion now for the right arm, left hand moving down the arm to finger tips and flick off.
10. Repeat this only once more for the left arm. *(Twice on left hand side and once on right hand side).*
11. To finish, return your hands to the prayer position and give thanks.

This technique is an excellent way to cleanse the body of unwanted energy. A further extension of this technique, is to imagine that you are wearing white gloves that act like magnets for your stress, tension, worry and lower emotions. As the hand brushes across the body, it draws this lower energy in the form of soot, dirt or grime. Once your hand is at the hip, the glove is black with this unwanted energy. Then flick your hand, with the intention of transmuting this lower energy into a positive energy. For example, one can imagine this energy landing on the floor as precious stones, diamonds, pearls or other symbols. Then place your hand on the other side of the body which has a new white glove, ready to draw out the lower energies and purify the body, mind and emotions.

Reiki Shower – A technique for cleansing the body and increasing energy with Reiki

Reiki Shower is a technique for showering yourself in Reiki energy, which has a cleansing effect on the body and increases your vital energy. This technique is also an excellent way to cleanse your energy field (Aura) of lower or unwanted energies. This method comes from Horishi Doi with added visualization techniques by the author.

The Technique:

1. Stand or sit comfortably. Close your eyes. Breathe slowly and naturally and let all thoughts and ideas just go by without evaluation.
2. Place your hands in prayer position, hands folded at heart level, with your fingers pointing away from your body at a slight angle. Calm your mind and say silently *"I will begin Reiki Shower now".*

3. Now reach your hands, high above your head and connect to the fullness of the Reiki energy. (*You can imagine your body is filling with energy*). Imagine that you are touching a vast field of energy and light. You can also imagine this like an enormous planet, representing the unlimited power of the Reiki energy.

4. Now imagine that you are receiving a shower of Reiki energy, over and through your entire body. Feeling the fullness of this energy, slowly move your hands down the front of your body, palms facing you. Your hands are bathing you in Reiki energy, cleansing all areas of imbalance and purifying all disease, negative emotions, and thoughts. All of these lower energies are transmuted or seen moving down your body and out the soles of your feet, never to return. One imagines the earth beneath us crack open slightly, absorbing the lower energies and excess Reiki energy. Feel this flowing over you. As it does, it takes with it all of these lower energies down into the earth, where they are transformed by all the power of nature.

5. If you have an area in particular which requires more time, spend as much time as is necessary bathing this area.
6. On the next in-breath, bring your hands out to the sides of your body and as you breathe in, imagine you are drawing in more purifying energy over your head.
7. Now on your out-breath, wash your hands over your body again as per step 4.
8. Continue this practice for several minutes or until you feel purified and cleansed of any lower energies. Once you feel that you are full of positive healing energy, return your hands in the prayer position and give thanks.
9. To finish, imagine that the earth below you seals up once again and you are left feeling pure and clear.

- NOTE: This is an excellent technique to do under a waterfall or in the shower, imagining the water is the Reiki energy and that it not only moves over your body but through it, cleansing all areas of imbalance.

22
The Path of Humility

Reiki and the Path of Humility

One of the easiest Reiki traps a new teacher can fall into, is Pride. When we make the transition from being a student to being a teacher, we can have wrong views. We might think that we have achieved a level of status, or that we have arrived at a final destination in our spiritual journey. We gain ideas like: *"now I am a Reiki Master, now I am the teacher"*. We might also think: *"Before I was a practitioner and I had special powers, now that I'm a Master, I'm even better"*. Sometimes one may generate an overly holy nature, where what I call 'spiritual snobbery' unfolds. Here, the teacher considers themselves higher or greater than his or her spiritual friends and begins to show elitist tendencies like: *"I know more about Reiki than you"*, or *"soon I will become enlightened"*. Our egos have many subtle ways of seducing us into believing that we are somehow superior in spiritual accomplishment, by means of our level three attunement.

To quote Chogyam Trungpa Rinpoche: *"As long as one's approach to spirituality is based upon enriching ego, then it is spiritual materialism, a suicidal process rather than a creative one"*.

In truth, there is no glory in being a 'Reiki Master'. The path of Reiki is one of service and humility, but you would be surprised at how many Reiki Masters run around boasting about their healing abilities and seeking praise and validation from others.

Those who are awake do not seek praise, nor wish to be seen. They practice anonymously, have a humble disposition and seek to benefit beings wherever they can. They do not wish acknowledgment for their efforts, nor wish to be given titles or position above others. Those who are awake find satisfaction from seeing the joy that comes from their healing activity.

During my training in Medicine Ways, my mentor used another colourful term to describe this strange behaviour. He called it *"Shamanic Fever"* – A highly contagious condition, where one deludes oneself into thinking that they have instantly achieved a heightened level of enlightenment. Here, all experiences arising in the mind are a sign of their own level of attainment and where others should reverently acknowledge their enlightenment. Unfortunately, this leads to further outbreaks of Shamanic Fever, *(delusions)* and certain other individuals exhibit the same symptoms.

Some other ways we can fall down are with our students. As soon as you take on the role of being a teacher, there will be some students who will immediately place you on a very high pedestal. Students like this will claim that you have all sorts of super-natural abilities and give you an immediate 'God-like' status. As a teacher, it is your responsibility to your students to gently bring them back to reality. One of the most effective ways is to walk your talk and act with humility.

So the question beckons: *"how do we cultivate a humble disposition?"*

Some of the more useful ways of averting these kinds of impressions is by maintaining a level of equality with others. Whenever you address a student, either take an equal position or when required, the lesser role. If they are standing, sit down and speak with them, or if they are in a chair, sit on the floor. Do your best to hold up the mirror and reflect back to the student, so they might be able to be self-empowered, self-reliant and have the ability to help themselves. Naturally offer what sound advice you can muster from your own experience, but be wary of those who approach you from a place where you are suddenly in the parent role, being 'Mum or Dad' for the student and telling them what they should or should not do.

In Buddhism, one of the eight training precepts for monks is to undertake the training rule to abstain from using high or luxurious seats or beds. Now, this may seem an odd precept for monks, but as with many teachings, it has an outer and inner meaning. If one was to view this precept outwardly, then one would be mindful not to either sleep nor sit on a high bed and instead be close to the earth. The inner meaning however, reveals much about the teaching of humility. One is then mindful of the ways that we might place ourselves higher than others in our views, actions and in our speech.

From a personal point of view, ways of watching your ego can take the form of selfless acts of kindness and service to others, without desire for recognition or something in return.

One can also regularly dedicate all positive benefit from any activity to the welfare of all living beings.

The following is a prayer or aspiration to subdue pride.

Say to yourself each day. *"I offer all positive actions, all past and present, all my possessions, all that I am, my life, my body, I give it all away for the benefit of all that lives. May I be an instrument of the divine and may all my future actions be in the useful service of humanity. May I surrender to the path of healing and service, and may I be a fit vessel for the benefit of others."*

This prayer is only an example, so it is best to write your own aspiration for yourself and in a way which is meaningful to you. Prayers or aspirations like this are a direct way of giving up pride and can greatly benefit ourselves in cultivating a humble disposition, provided we choose to embrace this in a genuine and authentic way.

Further to this, you can also attend to your unruly ego by engaging in some regular activity which is involved in community service. Or even better, find a good teacher to assist selflessly. In Buddhism this is called 'Karma Yoga'. This is where a student will attend to a Lama's needs. Selfless actions to a realized being have a direct positive effect on the aspirant and many accumulated negative impressions can be liberated through these selfless actions. If you can't find a good and kind teacher to assist, donate some of your money and time to a worthwhile cause. However, this cause should be free of personal benefit to your self.

23

Walking the talk and spiritual practice

Living by Example

By being a teacher of Reiki, we are called to better ourselves and to be mindful of our conduct. We also need to be honest with ourself and do the necessary work to heal our personal issues. Students (especially new students), look to their teacher as an example of the teachings. A Reiki teacher must therefore be clear on how he or she presents themselves and not only talk in a moral and ethical manner, but lead by example.

As a teacher, when you give advice or prescribe a practice to a student, you must have practiced these methods first yourself. Nothing speaks stronger than one's personal and direct experience. If you have no inner understanding of what you teach, your students will not only see the transparency of your claims, you will be unfit to adequately answer their questions, when they arise.

Always take the necessary time with a particular Reiki practice before giving it to others. If you find yourself in a position where you are sharing new information and have had little time to practice, tell your students then at least everyone will be clear, and no misconceptions on your level of experience will need to be raised.

In many spiritual traditions, the emphasis is always on the repetition of practices which, through such repetition, strengthen the positive impressions on the subconscious mind.

Like using a pick axe to break through a frozen lake, it is only by the constant repetition of chopping in one place, that we will break through. So it is with spiritual practice.

As a teacher of Reiki, Reiki is your spiritual practice, so it is vital that one attends to this. Whether this is simply making the time to give yourself Reiki each day, or some form of energy enhancing meditation, mastery comes through regularity and repetition.

Regular practice can be likened to building a single story house made of steel, rather than a high tower with foundations of mud.

For many of us, we all have numerous tasks to attend to each day and it is sometimes impossible to dedicate hours to practice each day. But if we consider that it is the goal of quality, not quantity that matters in our regular practice, then five minutes of pure intention and the calm abiding which follows, is far more beneficial than 1 hour, if our minds are full of distraction, agitation and confusion.

"Better to live one moment completely awake then to live a hundred years in ignorance" – Everyday Buddha

The right view with practice is to make your daily practice a joy. Spiritual practice is a gift to your mind. Your Spiritual practice is also entirely your responsibility, as no one will ever do it for you. It is completely up to you and what you do in this life will determine your future self.

The four reasons which motivate us to practice

The first reason which motivates our mind to attend to a spiritual practice, is to think about the precious opportunity we have right now. We have a blessed human existence and we have the ability to use our senses to better ourselves. In Buddhism, this is considered the best possible situation, for we have a precious human body. This precious human body enables our self to learn and practice the Dharma. A human life is also considered precious, because it is hard to obtain and so easily lost, therefore we should practice diligently right now, while we have the chance.

The second motivating principle is to think about Death and Impermanence. Nothing is permanent in this world, everything is subject to change. The only thing that is lasting, is our minds and we have the rare opportunity in this life to make the right changes to strengthen this mind. We also never know when death will fetch us away and if we have made no provision for our transition, then where will we be? If we make provision in this life, it is like we have packed well for a long journey, we will have what we need and this will assist us in our future existence.

The third motivating principle is that of cause and effect or *'karma'*. Everything we do, say and think creates our future. Therefore, if we give up negative actions and devote our time to spiritual practice and the practice of mindfulness, we will secure a path which leads to liberation.

The fourth motivating principle is to recognise the flaws of conditioned existence. We are constantly caught up by our desires, attachments, pleasures and possessions. We cannot take any of these things with us when we die and none of them will ever bring us lasting happiness and liberation, because everyone is subject to old age, sickness and death. Seeing there is no real refuge to be found in the conditioned world, we seek to know our minds and joyfully strive to liberate our minds through spiritual practice.

So, take a moment now to review what it is that you do in your life as a spiritual practice. I ask you to put down this book and write a list of your spiritual practices. It need only be one, but if you have none, then perhaps it is time to search for at least one.

If you happen to be working with a spiritual practice, review the results. If no visible results have occurred, then one of two things is wrong. Either your practice is not the right one for you (in which case find a new one), or you are not practicing correctly. The thing is to start and if you can find an accomplished teacher who you can trust to guide you in your spiritual practice, then more the better.

24
Teaching Reiki

Public Speaking and Group Facilitation
One of the inevitable consequences of teaching Reiki is that of public speaking. It has been said that fear of public speaking rates in some peoples' minds as second to fear of dying. As extreme as this may seem, for some it is a reality.

In the west, many teachers choose to give an introductory lecture on Reiki. If you find yourself in this situation, some points to consider are as follows:

Overcoming nerves
The first thing to do is to calm your nerves. If at all possible, find 10 minutes before the talk to give yourself Reiki, and ask yourself the question, *"Where in my body do I feel my anxiety?"* Then place your hands there and direct Reiki. Whilst giving yourself Reiki, do some deep breathing. Visualize yourself giving an excellent presentation. Quickly walk through the presentation in your mind, listing off the key points.

Now, affirm that you will succeed and imagine the audience applauding your closing statement. If you feel nervous, don't point this out to the group, more often than not they will probably not even notice. Drawing attention to yourself in any negative way should be completely avoided. The way you see yourself is the way others will see you, so convey a confident and bright, likeable appearance and don't forget to smile.

Preparation
The key to a successful presentation is preparation. One of the best ways of preparing your talk is to write it out on single or multiple cards. Include all of the topics you would like to cover. List these into

categories. These categories should be written as simple questions which you will give an answer to.

For example: *What is Reiki? Where does Reiki come from? What are the benefits of learning Reiki?*

When we have a clear question as a marker, we can proceed, as we have a point to focus our discussion on.

The beginning, the body and the conclusion

The beginning of a talk consists of introducing yourself and thanking your audience for coming to see you. Next, one should make a definitive statement of why you are here. For example: *"Tonight I am going to present to you an informative discussion on the benefits of Reiki and how you can benefit from its practice"*. The beginning part of your presentation should be 10 percent of the total presentation time.

Give a break down of the topics you would like to cover in the discussion, and keep this to 5 or 6 topics.

The body of your talk will take the longest part of the evening and should logically cover all of the topics you mentioned in your introduction. This part of the talk should be 80 percent of your total presentation time and should ideally include a question and answer part. This keeps your audience active, as questions spark new directions in a presentation.

Finally, we have the conclusion. Review what you have covered. This part contains a similar amount of time as the beginning, roughly 10 percent of your total presentation time. In your conclusion, make a clear call to action, which might be something like: *"I want to thank you all for listening to me tonight, and if you would like to know more, I will be available after the talk and will be happy to speak with you personally. If you have an interest in our classes, we are taking registrations directly after the talk. Thank you once again."*

You may also like to make a closing statement like: *"If you only take one thing out of our discussion tonight, let it be this: The opportunity to heal yourself and others is your birthright, the choice of reclaiming it lies in the palm of your hands"*.

When preparing for a presentation, gather all the information you wish to present. Know your subject well and remember that you probably know more about what you will be presenting, than anyone else in the room.

Additional tips for giving great presentations

Know your audience. If possible, arrive at your talk with enough time to greet people as they arrive. Remember to smile, introduce yourself and you will have members of your audience already on your side.

- Remember to ask questions. Nothing engages an audience more than to give them something to do.
- **Utilize humour.** Tell a funny personal experience with Reiki, and remember your personal story is better than someone else's.
- **Begin on time.** If you wait more than 5 minutes after the start time, the people who arrived on or before the start time will begin to feel betrayed.
- **Remember peoples' names.** During question time, ask the person to give their name, then repeat the question, including the person's name. You will instantly validate the individual and give their question importance.
- **Praise Questions.** When someone presents a question, thank them for asking it and acknowledge the validity of their question.
- **Establish eye contact.** When giving your presentation, be sure to try and make eye contact with others in the room and do not only favour the ones who smile or nod at you. Everyone should have equal eye contact from you, especially if they are asking a question.
- **Use Body Language.** Become aware of your posture and use body language. Use your hands to express your point. If you just sit or stand there and never move, your audience will have a harder time keeping their attention on you. Make a point of using your body and facial expressions to engage your audience.
- **Beware of** *'er', 'ah', 'okay', 'umm',* **and** *'you know what I mean?'* Remember to breathe and use pauses in your speech, so you won't fill in the pauses with one of the above 'fillers'.
- **Regulate your voice.** Next time you watch a news broadcaster, notice their voice and how it changes in tone and variety. Try to use voice changes, but keep your own personal style and be authentic.
- **Smile.** Smiling is a universal symbol that everyone loves. Remember to use it often. At worst, everyone will wonder what you've been up to.

Remember these points and you will be well on the way to giving an excellent presentation.

Reiki Classes and the number of participants

When one decides to run a Reiki class, it is worth considering the size of the class. Ideally, you do not want to have a class that is too small, such as where it is only the teacher and the student, as this makes it hard to practice Reiki and to gain a wider view of experiences. Drawing from my personal experience, a minimum class size should be of two participants, even if this is an existing Reiki practitioner, reviewing to be a 'spare body' for the practical work. On the other hand, an overly large class can have its disadvantages. When some teachers offer Reiki classes to sixty or more at a time, the students have little time for personal contact with the teacher and a great deal of group intimacy is lost.

In the case of larger classes, it is ideal to have one or more assistants. This way if anyone begins to produce emotional baggage, the assistants can attend to the persons' process and the teacher can continue teaching without too many interruptions.

An ideal class size has the added elements of group safety, intimacy and disclosure.

Generally speaking, groups of 4 to 14 people seem to work best in terms of creating an openness and safety in the group. When there is more than these numbers, careful consideration should be put in place, with regard to supporting participants or having other Reiki teachers assisting in the class. Although it is unlikely that the Universe will allow more people than is necessary for you, it is worth considering just how many people you feel comfortable teaching at one time. Groups of smaller numbers create safety and with safety, students can drop their masks and reveal their vulnerabilities.

Attention spans and taking breaks

Most people in a class environment have a twenty minute attention span. With this in mind, it makes good sense to plan a workshop according to segments. These should follow into one another and make the class interactive. For example, when demonstrating the Reiki hand positions, follow by asking one of the participants to demonstrate on behalf of the group. If your students are practicing a hands-on healing session of one hour duration, in between sessions, create a brief time for sharing their experiences.

Besides having morning, lunch, and afternoon breaks, is not uncommon in a workshop to have several mini-breaks. Even if this is to have a glass of water, a little stretch or a quick question. All these things help keep the mind alert and grounded throughout the day.

Remember to be sensitive to your students needs, encourage questions, sharing and feedback for the methods practised. It is also suggested to inform your students as to what is coming up next. This assists in creating a direction and flow in the workshop. If your intention is clear, the energy will follow and so will your student's attention and enthusiasm.

At times during a workshop, students may get that 'glazed look' in their eyes.

When purifying, they may experience boredom; agitation; emotional releases; and some physical discomfort. If possible, make concessions for these Reiki purifications and if a student does not wish to participate in an exercise, then allow them to take time out.

If they have understood the practice, they will have time later on to practise. Alternatively, you may give the student in question additional homework to catch up on missed practices, or simply take some time in follow up meetings to assist in their understanding of the material.

In the case where the student has missed too much, it is perfectly acceptable to request that the student reviews the workshop at a later date. No additional fees should be charged in this case. Your obligation as a teacher is to teach your students to the best of your ability and not only this, but to nurture this experience after the class.

The students' obligation is to learn, to practice and to follow up on your recommendations.

Finding your style

When teaching Reiki to others, it is important to cultivate your own personal style. This will naturally begin to develop more and more, through teaching classes.

It is important to make Reiki your own, yet still hold sacred the Reiki tradition and maintain the methodology of your lineage, without removing or inventing new material. As you progress through your teaching career, you will be shaped by your experiences. The more you teach, the more these interactions with students and the Reiki energy will have an effect on you as a teacher. In time, the uniqueness of your personal style will begin to shine through and others will be drawn to you because of it.

Building confidence

When stepping into the role of teacher, confidence in our ability to offer something worthwhile is most helpful. Remember, the very reason a student is drawn to you, is because of sympathetic resonance. Like attracts like and your students are attracted to you due to karmic forces, playing out in physical reality. So, if you feel you lack the ability to offer something worthwhile the Universe, by default, has already determined you to be a fit vessel.

A clear indication that one is not fit to teach is that your students simply won't show up. Provided one has the correct address, then the very fact that students seek you out, even if they are not consciously aware of the inner process, speaks loudly of your ability to offer something of value. This is the first acknowledgement of your value as a teacher of Reiki.

Secondly, when wrestling with our worthiness and self-confidence, we should take on the attitude that we are an expert. Even if we feel we lack a complete understanding and accomplishment, one should as they say, 'fake it until you make it'. You must act as you would become.

Let me quote the Buddha: *"All that we are is the result of our thoughts; and with our thoughts we make the world. If a person speaks or acts with harmonious thoughts, happiness follows, like one's shadow, never leaving."*

Transference and projection

Often, there is the expectation placed on a teacher by the student, that as a teacher they must be perfect or have attained some level of enlightenment. This of course, can be dangerous. When unrealistic expectations are placed upon a teacher by the student and these expectations are not met, trust is lost and this creates obstacles to true learning.

It is incumbent upon a teacher of Reiki to be able to recognise these projections and gently guide the student back on track.

Walking the talk involves being very honest with oneself and being transparent to ones' students. It is not necessary to slip into some persona of 'I'm the teacher' and act differently to how one ordinarily would.

25
Materials for Reiki Classes

Materials list

Running a successful Reiki class is not just a matter of turning up and "winging it", preparation plays an integral part. This includes what you need to bring to your class. Here's a check list which may apply:

1. Massage tables or mats.
2. Pillows and covers, or blankets.
3. Tea and coffee facilities for breaks.
4. CD player and music to play during the hands-on sessions.
5. Tissues/toilet paper.
6. Materials for a shrine/candle/flowers etc...
7. Class notes, reading materials and relevant information.
8. Whiteboard and marker for any additional notes and diagrams.
9. Reiki Certificates for the level concerned.
10. Ideally, access to pure drinking water.

Sourcing tables

If you are lucky enough to find a venue that already has massage tables, then half your troubles are over. If not, then you will need to source massage tables for your students to practice their healing sessions. When it comes to massage tables, this is not an area to cut corners. It is vitally important that the massage tables you use meet quality safety standards. The last thing you want is someone falling off or through a table and giving themselves an injury, not to mention setting yourself up for litigation. Most holistic magazines advertise massage tables, or you can also contact your local massage college. You may be able to hire tables if you are not in a position to purchase them. Another idea is to speak to the manufacturer. Some massage table manufacturers are happy for you to demonstrate their tables and perhaps sell them at a workshop, in exchange for their use. Use your creativity, most people like their products receiving free exposure, making this a happy situation for all concerned.

26
Sacred Space

Finding a venue

Finding the right venue for running your classes is so important. The space should reflect the type of work which you wish to take place in that room. Before confirming a venue, where possible, you'll need to view the premises and "feel it out."

Practical factors like noise, location, facilities and cost are important.

The following are some points to consider in finding a venue for your Reiki classes:

1. The venue should reflect a presence of tranquillity. If the space does not have this naturally, then you'll need to create that feeling. This can be achieved by first clearing the room from previous energies, using the Reiki symbols. You can also create a peaceful energy by creating a simple shrine, including a candle, some flowers or a plant, incense and the like.
2. Make sure the venue is in an environment that will give you adequate silence. Facilitating Reiki with heavy traffic and construction work next door does not lend itself to meditation and healing states of mind.
3. Be sure that disruptions like phones, or people walking into the venue do not occur. A '*do not disturb, workshop in progress*' notice and taking the phone off the hook, will prevent unnecessary disruption in your classes.
4. If you are teaching a class at home, make sure that any pets are removed from the class environment, as some people have severe allergies to cats and dogs. Be sure to use only a little or no incense in a workshop for similar reasons, or where possible check with your class participants first.

If you do intend to run Reiki classes from home, consider the personal boundaries of your house. Many Reiki teachers prefer to run classes outside of their home environment, for reasons of personal space and privacy. Ideally, you'll need to find a place which suits the kind of classes you intend to run. A venue outside your personal life is preferable.

Creating a Sacred Space

The following information provides some advanced methods for averting negative energy, as well as creating a wholesome energy field which will optimise your healing sessions and class environment. Included are some basic guidelines for clearing your home as well as an introduction to some of the basic principles of Feng Shui.

Disruptive Energies

When we look at our environment, we can categorise imbalances in two ways.

These are:

1. **Physical imbalance.** Including clutter; grime; disordered objects; the way things are arranged which cause clutter and disrupt energy flow.
2. **Previous energy.** Meaning energetic patterns; and residual energies.

Physical imbalance

One of the first things we need to consider is our outer environment. We can do all sorts of meditations and practices to purify and clear a space, however if the physical environment is in absolute chaos, then we are really making things hard for ourselves.

The first thing to address is clutter. Clutter has two forms. There is the clutter that we find from accumulating too much stuff and there is clutter in the form of basic untidiness. When we neglect to remove old and unwanted items, we do not allow the new to manifest in our lives.

If we have identified ourselves as having clutter in our lives, the first thing is to liberate it. By this I mean get rid of it. If we wish to have abundance and flow in our lives, one of the best ways of allowing new things to enter is through releasing the old. You cannot fill up a glass of water if the glass is already full. You first need to empty it.

Identifying clutter:

Some of the more common areas where clutter accumulates include:

- on top of and in your wardrobes
- on top of and in your cupboards
- under the beds
- in the garage
- in the attic
- on your desk
- in your computer and email inbox
- in your tool shed
- under your house
- in your pantry
- in your bathroom

Do any of these sound familiar? Perhaps it will be all of the above, or just a few. Either way, the next step is to sort your clutter into sections.

One way to proceed, is to place items in the following 4 categories:

1. Junk
2. Too good to throw away = give away
3. Worth keeping, but needs storing
4. Necessary on a daily level

Once we have identified these areas where chaos reigns, we can then take positive steps towards clearing them.

1. Getting rid of your Junk. Here, I suggest a heavy hand. Be realistic, ask yourself: *"Do I need this item and will I need it in one year or in five years?"* If you could replace the item and it is of little value, why keep it? The greatest of freedoms comes from the simplest of needs. Let this be your motto and get rid of all the old and tired things which no longer serve you. Remember to also clean your house thoroughly. If it is dusty, it holds old energy and should be cleaned.
2. Too good to throw away equals give away. Here, you can give your unwanted items to a charity or even have a garage sale. You may encounter a second hand store who would like some items, or simply give items away to someone in need.
3. If it is worth keeping, but you will not need it tomorrow or next week, find a place for storage which is neat and tidy. Placing items under your bed, unless they are specific to sleep, interfere with dream time.

Placing unnecessary items on top of your wardrobe come into the line of your vision when you wake. So it is before you sleep. Before you sleep and upon waking the first thing you'll see is clutter which is an affirmation to your mind supporting clutter in your life. Once it is stored, then you can access it anytime you need without it being a constant visual affirmation that you have clutter in your life.

4. The items which are necessary on a daily level should be neatly placed or stored in the surrounding space. One example I remember was a friends' work desk that had papers piled one foot high on either side. In the middle of the desk *(I suspect there may have been a desk under all that)* was a space no bigger than an A4 page for writing. I'm sure if he had a bigger desk, then he would have placed two piles of clutter either side. The simple solution was to get a filing cabinet. As a result for the first time in years, he saw the wood of his desk. Subsequently, his work productivity improved from this simple action.

Previous energy

Once we have sorted out the clutter in our physical environment, we can then consider the subtle energies in our environment.

These energies many include accumulated negative impressions; stagnant energy; and old thought forms which have not been cleared. This type of disruptive energy has no separate, outside consciousness, rather, it refers to stagnant energy, which is the direct result of impressions left behind. Have you ever sat in an antique chair, or slept in another's bed? When something is used on a regular basis, these objects become imbued with the person's vibration. For example, if someone used a space to facilitate emotional release work and during the process, the person releasing it expressed tremendous amounts of anger, the person who would be next to use the space would be walking into a space with old disruptive energies.

In order to preserve a peaceful space, these old impressions need to be cleared.

The following are a number of ways of removing old and disruptive energies or thought forms, as well as accompanying methods for enhancing the positive energetic qualities of a room.

Smudging and purifying a room

Smudging is used in many cultures and combines the use of burning herbs known for their clearing and positive enhancing qualities. Popular herbs for smudging a space are sage; sandalwood; sweet grass; lavender; juniper; and cedar wood. However, if you do not have these on hand, a stick of good quality incense will also suffice. Be sure to open a window or door, to symbolically allow the lesser energies to leave the room.

Procedure:

Begin in the centre of the room you wish to smudge. Begin by passing the smoke over your own body. This is done from the crown of your head, to your feet. Then pass the smudge once around your body in a clockwise motion.

Once your own body has been cleansed, go to a corner of the room you are cleansing. Now walk the perimeter of the room, imagining that all of the lower energies, past and present, are being either transformed by your procedure, or are leaving the premises. As you walk, imagine that Reiki energy is beaming out of your palms, forming a protective shield around the whole room.

Once you have returned to the corner where you began, move to the centre of the room. At the centre of the room, place your hands in the prayer position with your hands folded at heart level. At this point, we can utilize our intention and use prayer and an invocation to bring in positive healing energies.

Pray and invoke in the following manner:

"I now call all of the highest healing energies of the Reiki system to be present within this room".

Repeat this request a second time. *"For the second time, I now call all of the highest healing energies of the Reiki system to be present within this room."*

And finally, repeat this request a third time. *"For the third time, I now call all of the highest healing energies of the Reiki system to be present within this room."*

At this point, we imagine that in all directions of space, thousands of miniature healing Buddha's appear, each emanating positive healing qualities, in all directions. Immediately, they simultaneously disperse blue lights, purifying all lower energies and generate healing energy within the room.

If one does not like to use Buddha forms, one can simply replace this visualization with blue spheres of energy and light.

Once these Buddha's have purified the space, they move towards us and merge with our body, filling it with their power, healing energies and light. We become totally one with their healing energy.

Now as we breathe in, this blue light increases within our bodies. In much the same way as we would see a balloon expand when blowing it up, so too when we exhale this blue sphere within, our bodies expand more and more.

Effortlessly, this blue light grows bigger with each exhale, effortlessly surrounding our bodies and increasing in size, until it has filled the entire room.

We imagine that any harmful or lesser energy is completely liberated through this practice and all things are transformed into the same vibration of healing energy.

Do this for five minutes or so or until you feel the whole room has been cleansed.

We finish by dedicating that whatever positive energy has been generated, be shared with all that lives, with the strong wish to increase happiness in the world.

Blessing Water

The use of water to symbolize purification and as a blessing is perhaps one of humanities oldest symbols. This is another useful way to bless a room or an object like your car, or anything which would benefit by receiving a blessing.

Take clean water and place it in a natural container, ideally made from crystal, however, any natural substance will suffice. Much in the same way as before, make strong requests for all the healing energies of the Reiki System to be present, this time within the water. *"I now call all of the highest healing energies of the Reiki system to be present within this vessel of water"*. Repeat this request a second and third time.

Now, imagine all of the healing energies expanding within the water, generating their positive healing energies in the water itself. It is like each drop contains a healing Buddha, which emanates the vibration generating wellness and all of its causes.

Your hands should be holding the vessel of water and you should also imagine that Reiki energy, in the form of blue light, is emanating from your hands into the vessel of water, filling it with light and healing power.

One does this for five minutes or so, or until it feels like the body of water is completely filled with healing energy.

We finish in the same manner as before, by dedicating any positive energy, which has been generated by blessing this water, to be shared with all that lives, so that there is great happiness in the world.

Then use this water to bless the room, using a branch or whisk to flick the healing water in all directions. Be sure to use the water in a sacred and reverent way and only use the water for this blessing purpose.

Note: When the water level becomes low, add new water and repeat the ritual for blessing.

Shrines and focal points

Another positive way to support the healing energies generated, is to maintain a shrine within the room. Shrines are a personal thing and need not be religious in their presentation. Some of the things which you might find on a shrine might include the following: A candle; healing water*; flowers or a plant – representing life and unfolding; incense; and an image which represents aspiration to a higher power. For this, you might choose a beautiful scene of nature or a Guru or Lama, or some image which conjures respect for divinity.

Ultimately, you can make a shrine in a way that is meaningful to you. In some tribal societies, offerings of alcohol, tobacco, sweets, or even a good pair of hiking boots are offered to represent the best things in life and for others, the offerings are a little more refined. Ultimately, an offering should speak to your sense of meaning, purifying and sincerity to all that is good. One should not only consider what is offered, but that state of mind which is carried into the offering.

We could think of this in the way we might give a gift to someone. We should first consider the gift and its appropriateness for the individual concerned.

Then we should consider our motivation for giving the gift. It matters not only what we do, but why we do the things that we do. It also matters how we carry out these actions and the feeling we bring to it, as these factors all bear results.

Think like this when you make an offering and you will experience the true benefit of the practice.

---

* From the previous exercise for blessing water.

27
Reiki Manuals and Certificates

Compiling your manuals

Most Reiki teachers like to supply their students with notes on the practices and methods for each Reiki level. Other teachers prefer to give Reiki classes completely as an oral tradition. If you intend to give handouts, then the K.I.S.S philosophy *(keep it simple, stupid)* will serve you best. Decide what is most important with regard to each Reiki level. Placing information in point form is a good idea, as it makes your material more user friendly.

As you grow with Reiki, perhaps your views about the way it should be taught will also change. There is no harm in updating your information, in light of your personal experiences.

Another important point to mention is to research your subject. If you intend to have a broad view of Reiki and be equipped to answer those 'curly questions', you need to know as much as you can about Reiki.

Sourcing certificates and practitioner qualifications

Having an acknowledgment in the form of a certificate for ones level achieved in Reiki, adds credibility to your students' practice and yourself as a teacher of Reiki.

If you intend to run Reiki classes, you should issue your students with a certificate upon completion. Whether a student receives a certificate of participation, or a certificate of completion (in the case of the training requirements and clinical practice), a word of advice is to pay good money for a professionally designed certificate.

Throughout my training in various modalities, I have received some awful looking certificates. These are the kind you'd rather file in your drawer, than display on your wall. In my opinion, you want your students to have a professional looking Reiki certificate. If you create a certificate that they will want to place in their practitioner room, others will see this certificate, which will add credibility to their training and ultimately, to you as their teacher.

28
Money and Value for Teachers

Reiki Fees and Charges for Teachers
With regard to workshop fees, it is important not to overcharge, but especially important not to undercharge for your services. In western society, we have the conditioning – *"you don't get something for nothing"*, or *"there's no free lunch"*, as the saying goes, so why shouldn't these concepts apply to the spiritual life?

A common teaching in Buddhism is the concept of 'Dana'. Dana refers to donation. In many western minds, the idea of a donation can mean throwing some spare change, so with this in mind, it is a realistic point to charge a fixed price for training others. In this way, you will protect the integrity of what you are offering, pay the bills and be able to continue your classes in a sustained way.

Supplementing your income with other work is also a very practical step, unless you intend to teach Reiki fulltime and make it your only source of income.

Assessing each person's situation is also a good thing to do. In this way, no one is turned away from the teachings. One may have to work hard to learn and make sacrifices, yet it is through these sacrifices that one truly appreciates what they have gained.

With regard to IOU's, I suggest you avoid these kinds of arrangements. I can not count the amount of times in the past where an IOU has caused some kind of problem, as the person concerned may not be able to stand by their obligation. This is not always the case, but it is considered a better alternative for a new student to wait until they do have the means to attend a class, rather than paying off a debt. If circumstances change, (and life certainly has a habit of doing this), then we may find ourselves in a difficult position when students owe us a debt.

When it comes to teaching Reiki, boundaries should be set around the subject of money. The more money being invested, the more the boundaries need to be observed. Be clear on what you are offering and be clear on what you ask for your services.

If you are running workshops and expect people to turn up on the day, nothing guarantees attendance like a non-refundable deposit. Even if it is only a $50 deposit, the money given is a statement of the prospective students' commitment. It is all too easy to change our minds, make excuses, or sabotage our healing journey when we have made no clear commitment in the form of money.

Deposits should be paid at least seven days before the workshop. Considering the expenses it takes to run a seminar, it makes sense to ask for a deposit before the seminar begins. The balance of the students' fees should be paid in full on or before the day of the workshop. This asks the student to put their intention to learn in focus.

Placing value on your time and experience comes down to one's personal motivation and financial situation. For some, a few hundred dollars is a walk in the park, for others, it means months of savings and doing it tough, making sacrifices to make the funds available. Ultimately, each person is in a different position financially, therefore, you need to be flexible and take each person's situation into account.

When we come to promoting our Reiki workshops, we can have the best intentions and indeed be a highly skilled teacher, but this does not mean a great deal if no one knows you exist. It is therefore important to put yourself 'out there'.

Many teachers I know embody the practices of Reiki, yet when it comes to selling themselves and the benefits of Reiki, they have only a vague idea of how to do this.

You will find that many of the marketing tools from section one of this book will aid you in your teaching endeavours, but here are a few more things for teachers to consider.

Know what you are offering

Before we can promote what it is that we do, we firstly have to define and decide on what we do and what we are offering.

A good exercise is to write a list of what you teach during a Reiki workshop. List all the things that you offer and why. In doing this, you will be able to see exactly what you are offering to people. This exercise also clarifies what you have to offer and often triggers whatever might be missing.

Here are a few questions which you may wish to ask yourself, regarding to this initial process:

1. What do I offer in a Reiki workshop?
2. What are the benefits of these practices?
3. Who is my target audience and do I wish to target special interest groups?
4. Who will benefit from these practices?
5. Which of these sections are easy for me to teach?
6. Which areas do I need to work on?
7. How can I improve these problem areas?

Once you have identified your workshop content, you'll need to start to plan your workshop. You may wish to model your workshops on your initiating teachers' procedures, or you may wish to create a new format. Whichever way you choose, make sure there is adequate time to cover the material and sufficient time for breaks, answering questions and time to integrate the material learnt. There is no merit in trying to pack two days material into a one day workshop. Give your students plenty of time and a chance to practice the methods taught during the workshop.

Getting feedback

Receiving feedback from workshop participants is invaluable. If there are areas in your presentation that need finetuning, then your students are an excellent gauge.

Most people feel uncomfortable giving criticism about a workshop directly, so a good way to get around this, is to offer a simple questionnaire, which grades various aspects of the workshop. This need only be a simple tick the box questionnaire.

Being organized and cultivating your database

Setting up a database is essential. Having a database means you'll know how many people have learnt Reiki with you and you'll have their details on hand, whenever you need to send out information regarding further training and support groups. Ideally, you will want your students to follow through with learning additional Reiki levels. We call these people *"repeat offenders."* All jokes aside, students who train in First Degree Reiki with a teacher, will generally follow through to Second Degree, provided they feel that they have received quality training.

A teacher can support and nurture this process by offering on-going reminders of upcoming workshops, offering practice times for students and encouraging students to review a workshop at anytime for a small donation.

You may also wish to offer some form of community service for Reiki. This can take the form of a healing clinic or in-house service programmes, through hospitals, for example. In these ways, a student will see tangible uses of Reiki and how it can directly benefit themselves and the community.

Another excellent and instant tool is the internet. Setting up an email address book for your students is a sure way to access a great many people with one click and is also very cost effective.

29

The Principal Components of Reiki Seminars

The following is an overview of what is traditionally taught in the first, second, and third Degree seminars of traditional Reiki. Here, I will illustrate examples from the Japanese Reiki tradition which may be used, depending upon your particular style, when teaching Reiki classes.

For the First Degree *(Shoden)*, Second Degree *(Okuden)* and Third Degree *(Shinpiden)*, each seminar is broken up into 4 sessions of 3 hours. This makes each seminar 12 hours in duration, for each level.

In most cases, these classes are taught over a weekend, however, some teachers may offer these classes over four evenings, or over four weeks one session per evening, per week.

The Principal Components of a First Degree Seminar (Shoden)
Traditional Japanese Reiki *(Dentou Teki Usui)*

Session 1 (3 hours):
Introduction to Reiki – overview of the training
Participants introduce themselves and share their expectations and hopes for the training.
Instructor introduces themselves and gives the participants an overview of their Reiki history and experience.
Instructor explains the Reiki attunements and gives the first of four Reiki attunements given at the First Degree.
Instructor teaches the first of two energy exercises, these being: *Hikari no Kokyu-ho* (Breathing in the light meditation), and *Gassho Kokyu-ho* (Breathing through the hands meditation).
The Reiki history is explained, including up to date developments in

Reiki.

The students then practice a short, 20 minute Reiki treatment on one another.

Session 1 closes by each participant sharing their experiences.

Session 2 (3 hours):

Participants receive the second Reiki attunement and learn another three Japanese Reiki techniques. These include: *Kenyoku-ho* (The method of dry bathing), *Nentatsu-ho* (How to send a thought or wish with Reiki) and *Reiki Mawashi* (How to create a circuit of Reiki energy for oneself, or a whole group)

Participants are then shown how to give a full Reiki self-treatment and this is practiced for 30 minutes to 1 hour.

Session 2 closes by each participant sharing their experiences.

Session 3 (3 hours):

Participants receive the third Reiki attunement and learn another three Japanese Reiki techniques. These include: The *Gassho* Meditation (A meditation for concentration on the breath), *Chakra Kassei Kokyu-ho* (Chakra breathing meditation) and *Jakikiri Joka-ho*, (A practice to purify objects and rooms with Reiki energy).

Participants learn how to administer a full Reiki treatment on one another for 1 hour.

Session 3 closes by each participant sharing their experiences.

Session 4 (3 hours):

Participants receive the fourth and final Reiki attunement and learn another three Japanese Reiki techniques. These include: *Reiki Undo* (A method of body movement with Reiki), *Reiki Shower* (A purification practice using Reiki energy), and *Shuchu Reiki* (A method of group Reiki treatment).

Participants return the full Reiki treatment, given during session 3 for 1 hour on their partner.

The Reiki Principles are explained and session 4 closes by each participant sharing their experiences.

NOTE: Many of these practices and meditations mentioned are available on a guided Meditation CD by Lawrence Ellyard, titled: 'Reiki Samadhi'. For details visit: www.reikitraining.com.au

The Principal Components of a Second Degree Seminar (Okuden)
Traditional Japanese Reiki *(Dentou Teki Usui)*

Session 1 (3 hours):
Introduction to Reiki – overview of the training

Participants introduce themselves and share their expectations and hopes for the training.

Instructor introduces themselves and gives the participants an overview of their Reiki history and experience.

Participants receive the first of three Reiki attunements for the Okuden level.

Participants receive the Second Degree 'Power symbol' and have its use in Reiki explained.

Participants receive the second of three Reiki attunements for the Okuden level.

Participants receive the Second Degree 'Harmony symbol' and have its use in Reiki explained.

Participants receive the third and final Reiki attunement for the Okuden level.

Participants receive the Second Degree 'Connection symbol' and have its use in Reiki explained.

Session 1 closes by participants practising the three Reiki symbols, in pairs and in a group, as well as signing the symbols on paper to ensure accuracy.

Session 2 (3 hours):
Participants learn the first of two Okuden level techniques: *Byosen Reikan-ho* (Method of sensing imbalance with the hands) and *Reiji-ho* (Method of allowing Reiki to guide you in hands-on healing).

Participants practice both techniques on one another for 15 minutes per practice session, both giving and receiving (total 1 hour).

Participants learn the 5 Mudras which accompany the Second Degree and their use and application in Reiki.

Session 2 closes by each participant sharing their experiences.

Session 3 (3 hours):
Participants learn further Okduen Reiki techniques, these include: *Taden Chiryo-ho* (Method for removing toxins from the energy body), *Heso Chiryo-ho* (Method for Navel healing), *Gyoshi-ho*

(Method for healing with the eyes), *Koki-ho* (Method of healing with the breath), *Sei Heki Chiryo-ho* (Okuden method for sending a thought or wish), *Okuden Reiki Undo* (Movement meditation using symbols for healing), *Okuden Shuchu Reiki* (Method of group Reiki treatment using symbols), *Jiko Joka-ho* (Method of breathing to balance internal energies with toning) and *Uchi-te Chiryo-ho, Nade-te Chiryo-ho, Oshi-te Chiryo-ho*, (Methods of energy massage, including applied acupressure).

Session 3 closes by each participating in a short treatment session, practising some of the previously mentioned Reiki techniques.

Session 4 (3 hours):

Participants learn *Enkaku Chiryo-ho* (Method of distant healing).

Participants practice several variations of *Enkaku Chiryo-ho* including self distant healing; healing the inner child; sending Reiki to current or past issues; combining distant healing with hands-on healing; and the various uses of a proxy for distant healing. These being a photo; one's body; and an effigy, such as a pillow or teddy bear to represent the body of the person we wish to heal.

Session 4 closes by each participant sharing their experiences.

The Principal Components of a Third Degree Seminar (Shinpiden)
Traditional Japanese Reiki *(Dentou Teki Usui)*

Session 1 (3 hours):
Introduction to Reiki – overview of the Shinpiden training.

Participants introduce themselves and share their expectations and hopes for the training.

Instructor introduces themselves and gives the participants an overview of their Reiki history and experience.

Participants are guided through a short meditation on the Reiki lineage and founding teacher, Mikao Usui.

Participants receive the Third Degree Reiki attunement for the Shinpiden level.

Participants receive the Third Degree 'Empowerment symbol' and have its use in Reiki explained. Participants practice the symbol by signing it on paper, as well as reviewing the previous Reiki symbols from Second Degree. Participants give and receive a short Reiki treatment using the empowerment symbol.

Session 2 (3 hours):

Participants learn the Reiki Mudras which accompany the attunements for First and Second Degree.

Participants learn the preliminary practices prior to giving Reiki attunements.

Participants learn the method of *Reiju* (The Japanese Reiki method for giving Reiki attunements).

Session 3 (3 hours):

Participants learn how to give the Reiki attunements for the First and Second Degree (a total of seven separate Reiki attunements). Participants practice these attunement procedures many times, to refine their attunement ability.

Participants learn: *Ketsueki Kokan-ho* and *Zenshin Koketsu-ho* (Half and full body nerve stroke technique), and *Sekizui Joka Ibuki-ho* (The method for cleansing the spinal cord of karma).

Session 4 (3 hours):

Participants learn additional extensions for giving the Reiki attunements, including: self-healing attunements (3 methods), distant healing attunements (2 methods), and group Reiki attunements.

Participants review seven Reiki attunements in succession, to demonstrate their level of proficiency.

Seminar closes with a meditation on compassion and healing.

30
Generating Mastery

Motivation and personal integrity
As we have signalled before, being a teacher of Reiki holds a certain amount of responsibility, not only in the way we conduct our classes but how we live our daily lives as well. Therefore, it is important that a teacher of Reiki remain upstanding in their personal and spiritual lives.

Like it or not, when you are in the position of being a Reiki teacher, people will have an unspoken expectation of how you are, both inside and outside of the class room. Now I am not advocating that we adopt a holy façade, or act in a way which is overly spiritual, our aim is simply to be mindful of our conduct, our speech and our thoughts.

This in itself, should be the guiding principles of our lives 'being as we would wish to become'. Yet, when we are in the public eye, maintaining a spiritual demeanour affords a deeper trust by others, as you become a living example of a spiritual seeker.

Therefore, we should aspire to being a living example of the ideals presented within the Reiki system. We need to practice what we preach and walk the path of Reiki. By upholding the tradition of those who have walked this healing path throughout the ages, we honour their tradition and gain merit.

Working for others, benefit – the Way of the Bodhisattva
Above and beyond everything we do with the practice and teaching of Reiki, is that of the strong wish to benefit others through our healing activity. This is and should be our conscious motivation, to benefit all beings. In Buddhism, this notion is known as the path of the Bodhisattva.

A Bodhisattva is one who has achieved complete liberation from the bonds of suffering *(Samsara)* through the practice of benefiting others.

One achieves this through generating the mind of enlightenment (*Bodhicitta*). This is the mind that is dedicated to serve all beings, (not just the ones we like) through positive actions and service to others.

As the Dalai Lama says: *"Because we all share an identical need for love, it is possible to feel that anybody we meet in whatever circumstances is a brother or sister"*

The way to happiness is to give up our own self-cherishing and learn to cherish others. When I say give up self-cherishing, it does not mean have a low self-esteem, it means to give up our obsession with ourselves all our wants and desires; needs; material desires; what we like and dislike. If we focus on how we can benefit others in all that we do, say and think and treat all our relations like precious loved ones or with the same love a mother has for her child, we will be well on the path to lasting freedom.

The practice of Reiki is like this and this motivation should be at the forefront of your Reiki practice. Sooner or later, this will become evident through teaching others. When we pass on the Reiki attunements, we give others a priceless gift.

This is not only a boon for your spiritual path, it is a boon for others. Therefore, you become directly involved in cultivating spiritual merit, through your healing and teaching. Teaching Reiki becomes a path of the Bodhisattva. You would do well to remember this when teaching others and to always dedicate the benefit so that every being shares in this field of merit, by your sincere wishes to help all beings.

The great Indian Buddhist master Shantideva who lived in the 7th century, was famous for his teachings on compassion. If one wishes to gain a deeper understanding of what the path of compassion truly means, read *A Guide to the Bodhisattva's Way of Life, by Shantideva*.

The following is an excerpt from his teachings on compassion, to give you a taste of this deep wish to benefit others. Shantideva writes:

> May I be the doctor and the medicine, and may I be the nurse for all sick beings in the world, until everyone is healed.
> May a rain of food and drink descend to clear away the pain of thirst and hunger. And during the aeon of famine, may I myself change into food and drink.
> May I become an inexhaustible treasure for those who are poor and destitute; may I turn into all things they could need, and may these be placed close beside them.

The Intelligence of Reiki

The more we practice Reiki, whether teaching or giving treatments, the more we become like the energy. With on-going practice, we also tend to recognise that Reiki is an intelligent energy, meaning that as we open ourselves to the inner experience of Reiki, the more we surrender to the tremendous wellspring of healing, as it guides and flows through us.

This is being in alignment with the universal nature of Reiki. We become a conduit for the divine as it comes through us and into those we administer healing and Reiki attunements to.

Although it is important to use our healing practice in a ritualistic fashion *(going through the various stages of giving Reiki attunements)*, it is equally important that these methods only create a house for the Reiki energy to reside in. Reiki occupies this house, it is the resident within the energy structure of our bodies. Although it affects the house and imbues its blessing field to all the surroundings, the Reiki energy is not the house. So it is with our practice of being a conduit for this universal healing energy. Just like creating a beautiful setting for a guest at your table, know that your guest is the greatest teacher and deserves the upmost respect. Serve your master well and your master will serve you. The practice of teaching others is a privilege, as you act as a mid-way point between divinity and humanity.

Frank 'Foolscrow' one of the greatest holy men of the native American Indian Sioux nation, gave this advice to those who talked the spiritual path. *"You are to be like little hollow bones, so the blessings of the creator can flow freely through you."*

May we all become hollow bones, so that we can be that conduit for the blessings of Reiki to flow into and through us and out into the world to benefit all beings.

31
Teaching Teachers

Teaching teachers

As you progress with your experience of teaching the First and Second Degree Reiki seminars, so will your students. It is usually recommended that a Reiki teacher facilitates seminars in the First and Second Degree for at least 2 to 3 years, but ideally it is recommended that a teacher facilitates these seminars for a period of 5 years, before considering teaching one of their own students to become a teacher in their own right.

The main reason for this recommended length of time, is that it enables the teacher to gain valuable experience in the ways of teaching Reiki. You cannot be an example of how to be a teacher, if you yourself have little experience in teaching the material. Nowadays it is sad to see how this discipline is being dismissed, by those who are keen to teach their own students to be teachers, before they themselves are ready to do so.

If you are presented with an opportunity to teach another the teacher's level, first consider your readiness and contemplate the matter deeply, for you take upon yourself a tremendous responsibility. You become that students guide, so that they in turn will guide and initiate others.

Upgrade Reiki training

At the *International Institute for Reiki Training*, we offer upgrade Reiki training for existing Reiki Practitioners and Teachers *(Masters)*. Over the years, we have encountered hundreds of people who have received very little instruction and, in some cases, little or no effective energy transmission from their teacher. This leads me to think that there must be an enormous lack of quality teachers passing on the Reiki tradition.

Part of my intention in writing this volume, is to educate and raise the overall awareness of Reiki practice. My wish is to elevate and maintain the genuine Reiki teachings, to help prevent the decline of one of humanities greatest treasures.

Because Reiki is a lineage transmission, it is very important that a new student receives authentic Reiki training from a qualified Reiki Instructor. One needs a teacher who has received the correct transmission from their teacher and so on down the lineage, to provide the new student with an adequate Reiki transmission via the Reiki attunements.

Then one must also consider the quality of the information being presented in the form of methods. These are the various ways of administering a Reiki treatment, including the energy meditations and practice for higher Reiki development.

So, when someone comes to you with an interest in reviewing or upgrading their training as the case may be, it is important to first determine just what they know.

One would usually ask which form or style of Reiki they have learnt, and if they can provide their Reiki Teachers Lineage tracing back to the founder, Mikao Usui.

More often than not, when I interview a prospective student for upgrade Reiki training, I ask: *"Which style of Reiki did you learn?"* I invariably get the reply *"Usui Reiki"* Which leads me to ask: *"Yes, but which style of Usui Reiki?"* It is often the case that most practitioners have little knowledge of the fact that there are some 70 or more different styles of Reiki to date. Although there are approximately a dozen or so which are the more commonly known styles, many people are still quite uncertain of what they have learnt.

Once a general understanding of what the prospective student has learnt *(which may be a great deal or very little)*, one can then determine whether the student begins from the beginners' level, or intermediate level.

Most Reiki Instructors will usually recommend that an existing Reiki Practitioner or Master review the beginners and intermediate levels (First and Second Degree), in order to receive the Reiki attunements once again in the teachers style, as well as brush up on the methods from each level. This is an excellent way to determine the practitioners' level of proficiency and level of knowledge within each level of the training. Of course, if the person in question has some foundation in practice, then some discount may be offered as recognition of prior learning.

32
Liberating Reiki Myths

The following are a variety of modern Reiki myths, some of which span from the sublime, to the ridiculous. When we examine the human intervention of a sacred science such as Reiki, we need to consider that as human beings, we are subject to our own conditioned reality. This conditioning flavours the way we see the world and in many respects, represents a considerable amount of the Reiki Myths listed.

The following myths about Reiki actually come from a variety of Reiki Masters, who believe them to be true. As you will appreciate, some of these concepts are so amusing that when I heard them, I thought it was said 'as a joke'. The thing is, there are all sorts of people out there with all kinds of ideas and experiences. So, as a way to celebrate their 'uniqueness', let us take a walk down the Reiki mythological path.

Some of the following Reiki myths have been held to be true by many teachers, for many years and I do not wish to present any disrespect by disproving them, it is simply a matter of looking logically at how things are.

I invite you, the reader, to read through the following with an open mind and heart and to check these contentious items for yourself. That way, you can be your own guide.

Myth #1: You cannot give Reiki self-treatments when lying down.
- **The Rationale:** Because you are not grounded whilst lying down.
- **The Reality:** Applying self-healing is by no means restricted to your physical orientation. Reiki self-treatments can be given in any circumstance, whether this be seated, lying down or standing on your head, for example, when combining your Reiki self treatment with yoga! The idea that Reiki transmissions are limited to the feet being planted firmly on the ground has no effect whatsoever in

adminstering Reiki self-treatment.

Myth #2: If the fingers are spread out during a treatment, the Reiki energy will not flow.

- **The Rationale:** The fingers must be together to activate the Reiki energy.
- **The Reality:** Reiki energy flows, regardless of whether the fingers are spread out or together. One could say that if the fingers are spread widely, then this will affect a radiating quality to the energy, which will not only work on the area where the hands are in contact, but radiate Reiki energy to the surrounding areas. When the fingers are kept together, the effect is much the same however, the Reiki energy is slightly more concentrated in the placement of the hands on the body.

Myth #3: Reiki must be administered from the head to the feet and one must not go back to places already covered, after they have been treated during the session.

- **The Rationale:** If you go over previous hand positions, you will disrupt the bodies' energy flow.
- **The Reality:** Reiki can be applied with great results no matter which sequence is used. It makes no difference to the effectiveness of the treatment whether one commences a treatment from the head to the feet or from the feet to the head. If the practitioner then goes back to previous hand placements on the body, this can only benefit and further increase the amount of Reiki energy flowing into this part of the body. In no way does this cause a disruption to the bodies natural flow of energy.

Myth #4: If the hands are placed on a recipient's body and are not precisely in place, the Reiki energy will not flow.

- **The Rationale:** Reiki only works when the hands are placed in the positions which correspond to the sequence given. For example: the 12 treatment hand positions.
- **The Reality:** When we examine the many Reiki traditions, we find particularly in the Japanese systems, that the emphasis on sequential hand positions is not emphasized. Yet, even within the western schools where this myth was born, the placement of the hands bears no direct result in the transference of universal energy.

The use of a set sequence of hand positions was first established by Chujiro Hayashi, one of Mikao Usui's trained teachers, as part of a standardized form of treatment. The basis for this form of 'hand positions', was simply to make sure the practitioner placed their hands on all of the major organs and places of energy flow in the body. It makes no difference which sequence is used, or if some or all are included. Reiki works regardless and is as simple as: *'Hands on, Reiki on, Hands off, Reiki off'*.

Myth #5: You cannot do Reiki whilst you are asleep.

- **The Rationale:** Reiki only flows when the facilitators mind is conscious and awake.
- **The Reality:** Nothing could be further from the truth. Regardless of the practitioner's state of consciousness, Reiki energy can be transferred, whether the channel is conscious, in an altered state, or asleep, for that matter. Giving yourself Reiki whilst going to sleep is an extremely beneficial practice and, considering we spend approximately a third of our lives in this state, this is a tremendous opportunity to practice Reiki. If you have ever had the experience of someone falling asleep whilst giving you a Reiki treatment (as I have), you will know that this myth bears no factual basis.

Myth #6: You cannot apply Reiki energy to broken bones.

- **The Rationale:** Reiki will work so fast as to knit the bone, which may need to be re-broken and then re-set.
- **The Reality:** The myth about not giving Reiki to broken bones reveals a long standing misunderstanding of the healing effect of Reiki energy. Reiki does assist the bodies' natural ability to heal itself and does bring about relief for a variety of aches and pains. However, Reiki will not knit a broken bone during an initial first aid treatment. The rationale behind this myth comes from the concept that if someone had a badly broken bone which needed to be set by a physician, then between the time of the injury and receiving the treatment *(assuming weeks had not passed)*, administering Reiki would fuse the bone. This would then result in a re-setting, thereby breaking the fusion as a result of the Reiki healing. Reiki is fast working for pain relief and swelling but it is not fast acting super glue!

Unfortunately, this myth has now extended beyond the original view of bone fusing (which in itself is complete nonsense), to practitioners who encounter broken bones now avoiding treatment all together. A broken bone is a tremendously painful and shocking experience. I've managed to break a few in my time and the direct application of Reiki in this situation can have an enormous benefit, both in reduction of swelling and pain management.

The reality is that one should always apply basic first aid and consult the expertise of a trained and caring medical practitioner. One would also use an ice pack or similar, to prevent further swelling of the injury, as well as directing Reiki energy to the area of concern.

Never withhold your Reiki ability to someone in need. You would be doing them a tremendous dis-service, whilst preventing that person from urgent relief to their injury.

Reiki will always travel (no matter where the hands are placed) to the area of most need in the body.

Myth #7: You cannot give Reiki to women who are pregnant within the first 3 months of pregnancy.

- **The Rationale:** Reiki could trigger an abortion.
- **The Reality:** This myth is believed to be born out of the fear of litigation amongst Reiki practitioners. In the event a woman in the early stages of pregnancy experienced a natural miscarriage and the woman concerned was receiving Reiki treatments, the fear is that practitioner may be blamed for the miscarriage.

  Reiki energy is safe energy and in no way can it contribute to the loss of life. If anything, the administering Reiki during pregnancy aids both mother and baby, in numerous ways. The more Reiki is received during this time, the better for all concerned.

Myth #8: You should not give Reiki to anyone for more than one and a half hours.

- **The Rationale:** You can over energise a person and overload their energetic system, resulting in an imbalance in their energy body.
- **The Reality:** You cannot give either yourself or anyone else too much Reiki energy. Long treatments will not have any detrimental effect on the energy system. In fact, the opposite is practically guaranteed.

  Provided one is using what is regarded as sound traditional Reiki methods, the energy of Reiki will not overload a person's energy system. Those who have experienced 'Reiki Marathons' or group treatments administered by numerous practitioners can attest to the enormous benefits gained.

Perhaps one way to look at the ideal length of time for treatments, is to draw the analogy of our body being a vessel, which is being filled up with energy. Once a vessel is filled to the brim, it is not necessary to keep on filling it, because it is full. Much like our own bodies, with Reiki, once the person has received all the energy they need, it is not necessary to keep on giving Reiki to that person. If any side effects could be seen from over use of a Reiki treatment, the recipient may feel somewhat spacey, however, drinking lots of water and taking some time to come back to the planet soon remedies this feeling.

For the most part, people who receive a long treatment will feel like they could drift off into a relaxing sleep.

Treatment hint: Each person's body is like a container which needs to be filled to restore balance. Give the person what they need. Once the glass is full, complete the session.

Myth #9: If a person does not use Reiki, their ability will diminish and they will be required to be re-attuned to Reiki.

- **The Rationale:** The person will become un-attuned to the Reiki energy if they do not regularly practise.
- **The Reality:** I believe this myth sprung up as a way to encourage new students to practice. In reality, once a person has received the Reiki attunements from a qualified Reiki teacher, the energy will not vanish due to lack of practise by the individual. It can be said however, that if one does not practise regularly, then it becomes difficult to gain a sound relationship with the energy. Although the Reiki energy is 'on tap' 24/7, it is through daily practise that one builds confidence and ability. Even if we learnt a Reiki class years' ago and have not used the practices from the class since, the energy is still running in the background. If a student has had a long break from Reiki, then it is also advisable to review a Reiki class and even be re-initiated by the teacher concerned. Not out of necessity rather, that the attunements act as a positive blessing and open the student to greater amounts of Universal healing energy.

Myth #10: You cannot receive more than the standard Reiki attunements.

- **The Rationale**: Additional Reiki attunements will cancel out previous attunements and overload the bodies' energy system.
- **The Reality:** In some systems of Reiki, the practice of regular self-attunement or receiving additional attunements from the teacher is an integral part of spiritual development within the system of Reiki. As explained previously, the attunements give a blessing and bestowal of Universal healing energy, which can only be of assistance to our health and well-being. Perhaps this myth was born out of some teachers' desire to retain their students, so they would not learn additional Reiki levels elsewhere. In Japan's traditional Reiki Society *(The Reiki Gakkai)*, the transmissions of the Reiki attunements take place weekly, to increase the practitioners' relationship with the energy. Other Reiki traditions employ the use of group or multiple attunements to greatly increase the potency of the energy. Whichever tradition you follow, there is no harm and certainly many benefits to receiving regular attunements in Reiki.

Myth #11: Reiki Masters must make Reiki their only source of income.

- **The Rationale**: It is said to be a part of the Reiki Tradition.
- **The Reality:** This myth began with Mrs Takata *(a key teacher in the Western Reiki Lineage)*. It was supported by many Reiki Masters, who considered it essential that to be a 'Master' of the system, Reiki must be the only source of income. As a result, many have suffered greatly, as their financial resources rapidly dwindled. Not to mention the high fees charged by some teachers, making this requirement, for many, unachievable.

The result was that teachers stopped teaching, because they could not afford to live. It is quite acceptable to have numerous interests as a teacher of Reiki and to pursue worldly enterprises to support one's spiritual endeavours. Logical, isn't it?

Myth #12: You cannot give a Reiki treatment to a person who is wearing a pacemaker.

- **The Rationale**: It will affect the pacemaker, rendering it ineffective, due to Reiki's electromagnetic frequency.
- **The Reality:** There has been no proof to substantiate whether this myth has any basis whatsoever. Whether this concept derived from a faulty pacemaker, which at the time decided to give up on life, or whether it was a way to increase the dogmatic approaches some teachers insisted on taking, remains unknown. If indeed, Reiki targeted pacemakers over other electronic equipment, how does one propose a way to measure this fact?

    There is, in fact, no evidence to support that Reiki actually is electromagnetic in nature or for that matter, affects the normal function of pacemakers.

    One might then suggest avoiding the heart area of the client, however, as we all know, Reiki travels to the areas of concern. One might conclude not treating people who have a pacemaker. This of course, is no solution and if indeed practiced, would only serve to support an unfounded superstition.

Myth #13: You cannot apply Reiki healing to someone's crown Chakra.

- **The Rationale**: This will disrupt their energy flow.
- **The Reality:** Reiki is completely safe. In no way will it harm a person or disrupt their energy flow, if anything, it will only serve to enhance it. This myth I have heard in many circles for many years. One reason for its use stems from some religious eastern traditions, where one does not touch the crown of a person's head, however, this is only confined to their religious belief systems. Reiki is not a belief system, nor is it a dualistic energy that could cause a mis-alignment or interference with another's energy system. In most Reiki traditions, the attunements are given via the crown chakra and as has been proven time and again, Reiki attunements switch on ones' healing ability.

    If you have a particular religious belief that the crown of your head is not to be touched, then this is fine, however, one should be mindful that it is not a part of the traditional Reiki teachings.

Myth #14: You cannot do Reiki distance healing without the persons' permission.

- **The Rationale**: The person concerned must give consent.
- **The Reality**: It is often a courtesy to ask permission before giving Reiki to another distantly, however, this in no way should act as a limitation. When we consider what we are offering to another, then the benefit far outweighs the need for approval or consent. One of the fun ways to experiment with distance healing is to set up some blind experiments with someone you know, where the person you are administering the distance healing to is simply asked to lie down at a specific time and to notice what they are feeling, if anything, for the duration of the treatment. Some teachers use the example of driving a car when receiving a treatment. However, the Reiki energy would never place another individual in danger.

  The key point to remember is that permission is preferred, but not necessary when giving healing to another.

Myth #15: You cannot give Reiki to someone in a coma.

- **The Rationale**: The person concerned must give consent.
- **The Reality**: For similar reasons to the previous myth, this is yet another example where logic and reason have left the building.

Myth #16: You cannot give Reiki to someone who has died.

- **The Rationale**: The Reiki will bind the individual to this world.
- **The Reality**: One thing that never goes out of fashion is dying. Once a person has died, one can assist the mind stream of the individual, however, there are some parameters concerning the most effective use of Reiki in this situation.

  In my book *'Reiki Healer –A complete guide to the path and practice of Reiki' (Lotus Press)*, I give the precise instructions of how one may assist a dying person, using Reiki. The idea that a Reiki session, whether distant or hands-on, will bind a person from making their transition has no basis. In most cases, one can send distant healing from the period of the point of death and for the following 30 minutes, then from day three up to a period of 49 days[*]. Beyond this time, the mind stream of the dead one has most certainly moved on.

---

[*] Based on the teachings presented in the Tibetan Book of the Dead.

So, there is no harm in giving Reiki to someone who has died and it can, in fact, be most useful. Perhaps just as important is the healing and nurturing that can be given to loved ones who are grieving. Reiki is a wonderful and powerful way to assist in grieving and letting go of those who have passed on.

Myth #17: You cannot give Reiki to someone who is under anaesthetic.

- **The Rationale:** The Reiki energy will bring the person out of the anaesthetic during the operation.
- **The Reality:** Like many other unfounded belief-based myths, surrounding the application of Reiki and its effect on modern medicines, this superstition has no basis. I have even heard of patients advising their anaesthetist to be sure to increase the amount of anaesthetic, as they would be receiving a distant Reiki treatment during the operation. Thankfully, I have not heard of a case where an anaesthetist actually took the advice of the patient.

Reiki is a safe and intelligent energy, its use does not create a circumstance where it will place a recipient in danger. Likewise, adjusting or reducing medication without the consultation and guidance of a trained medical physician is another dangerous and reckless notion.

One example of this was a person who suffered from extreme epilepsy, who would have an explosive fit if his medication was altered. On the unfortunate advice of a Reiki practitioner, he gradually began to reduce his medication. What resulted was a serious fit which placed the individuals' life in danger. Fortunately, the patient's physician found out about his patient's activities and swiftly enforced his necessary medication. I believe the Reiki practitioner was also heavily reprimanded by the patient's family. A practitioner dabbling in the medication of their clients can not only seriously endanger their lives, but they could also see themselves being prosecuted for serious neglect and malpractice.

Myth #18: You cannot give an individual Reiki on the base Chakra.

- **The Rationale:** This will spark the Kundalini energy to rise.
- **The Reality:** The use of Reiki on the base of the body will not, in itself, activate a Kundalini experience and is completely safe.

Reiki of itself will not cause a Kundalini experience for the

186 The Ultimate Reiki Guide for Practitioners and Masters

recipient, nor for the practitioner. The application of Reiki to the base of the body is a beneficial practice, however one should place their hands above the area concerned and then only with the client's consent. A Reiki practitioner must adhere to appropriate levels of touch, so the breasts and genital areas are *(for obvious reasons)*, out of bounds. Unless the individual has specifically requested hands-on *(in the case of physical conditions for example, breast cancer)*, then only when both parties are comfortable may this occur.

If one was to use specific practices to raise the spinal energy (Kundalini) from the base of the body, then one would need to employ practices which include certain breathing exercises and body positions to generate a Kundalini outcome. One should never engage in Kundalini practices, unless under the close guidance of a qualified and experienced master.

Myth #19: You cannot give Reiki to another, unless you concentrate.

- **The Rationale:** Reiki energy only flows via concentration of the mind.
- **The Reality:** If this myth were true, then Reiki would fall into the category of being a belief based, dualist energy practice. The reality is that once a person has had their Reiki ability switched-on via the Reiki attunement procedure, the energy is flowing all the time. It is only our awareness which is not sure of its presence. Reiki certainly can be increased by our concentration and we will be more aware of this interaction if we focus our minds on the processes at hand.

   However, Reiki will also be effective if our minds are engaged in other activities. For example, whilst holding a conversation; watching television; eating a meal; sleeping, or during meditation practice. The use of our minds is one of the most beneficial things to cultivate and it is encouraged to enhance concentration and awareness whilst giving Reiki to oneself or others, but the results are not dependant upon it.

Myth #20: You can only sign the Reiki symbols with your dominant hand.

- **The Rationale:** Only your dominant hand has the ability to manifest the energy field of the Reiki symbols.
- **The Reality:** This myth stems from certain forms of Reiki, where

the attunement procedure in the Second Degree only attunes the
student's dominant hand with the Reiki symbols. Mikao Usui never
favoured one hand over the other, however, the understanding
that one side of the body is 'yin' *(passive)* and other 'yang' *(active)*
is present. This has no actual bearing on the signing of symbols.
Even if your initiating teacher for Second Degree only attuned your
dominant hand, the manifestation of the Reiki energy via the Reiki
symbols is a total body experience.

Myth #21: You cannot give Reiki to someone if you are unwell.

- **The Rationale:** The practitioner will become drained, or will transfer
  their ill-health to a person they are treating.
- **The Reality:** Not so. The first thing we must understand, is that
  when we are giving Reiki to either ourselves or another, we are not
  expending our own life-force energy. Reiki is an additional source
  of life-force energy. Counter to this myth, when one gives Reiki to
  another, the Reiki energy must first pass through the body of the
  practitioner, before it is passed onto another. If one is feeling depleted
  or unwell, a treatment will actually increase our own vital energy and
  state of mind.

  The second point is that one will pass their own illness to the
  person they are giving Reiki to. This is highly unlikely. Somatic
  transference, where one feels the symptoms of another, can and
  does happen during treatments, however, this is usually an indicator
  for the practitioner. In many Reiki traditions, specific methods are
  utilized to prevent these forms of energy transference and other
  indicators can be utilized by the practitioner.

  Another point to mention, is that one should always consider
  one's own personal health and energy levels. It is okay to say no
  to facilitating a Reiki treatment, when you could use a treatment
  yourself.

Myth #22: You cannot give someone Reiki on their spine.

- **The Rationale:** You may interfere with the person's natural energy
  flow.
- **The Reality:** Reiki is wonderful for backs and the spine is no
  exception. Reiki does not and should not include any manipulation
  of the spine, unless one is a licensed chiropractor, osteopath, or
  physiotherapist. Reiki, by itself, will have no adverse effect on a

person's spine. The other point concerning the interference of a person's energy flow has no basis. Reiki assists the bodies' natural energy to create a harmonious and balanced flow.

Myth #23: You cannot give Reiki to someone who is bleeding from a serious cut.

- **The Rationale:** Reiki will increase the bleeding.
- **The Reality:** The first rule in any first aid situation where a serious cut is involved, is to apply First Aid. Reiki in no way increases blood flow from a cut or wound. Reiki is an intelligent energy. It cannot harm, only heal. Surely, if one has a bad cut, then applying pressure, binding and elevating the wound, in a first aid situation is the first step. The second step is to call for medical assistance. Whilst the hands are on the area of concern, Reiki will naturally begin to flow. I have treated serious cuts on numerous occasions, both to myself and others, some of which have required stitches.

Through the direct application of first aid and the use of Reiki directly to the wound, I have personally, in almost every case, seen bleeding immediately cease and in some cases, wounds sealing. Reiki accelerates the bodies' natural ability to heal itself, it increases blood circulation however, increasing blood flow from a cut or wound is certainly not the case.

Myth #24: You cannot give Reiki to someone you are attracted to.

- **The Rationale:** Unknown origin.
- **The Reality:** This myth certainly took me by surprise. The student who told me, had no explanation on as to the mysterious reason behind this practice, however he had heard it was most important not to give Reiki to someone if you felt a strong attraction. Perhaps this myth stems from the view that one should be aware of ones sexual energy and not let this consume your healing session. One would, of course, adhere to the correct limits, whilst giving a Reiki treatment and in no way cross these boundaries as part of practice. That is why general codes of practice are considered. If this rule were true, no loving couple would ever be allowed to give their partner a Reiki treatment!

Is Reiki not a practice of love and kindness and a direct way to nurture and share with others? Reiki is a unique way of healing with touch, what could be more natural than that?

Myth #25: You cannot cross over your hands or arms when giving Reiki, either to yourself or others, nor should the feet be crossed when receiving a treatment.

- **The Rationale:** This myth suggests that if one crosses over one's hands or feet, this will close down the aura of the person administering the session, thereby blocking the flow of Reiki to the recipient.
- **The Reality:** Reiki is not based on polarities, so it makes no difference to the effectiveness or quality of energy being transferred, if the arms, hands, legs, feet, fingers or eyes are crossed! The energy will flow all the same, without effort or strain. Certain postures do affect internal energy flow, however, this is different to the Reiki energy flowing through the body. One should, where possible, be conscious of body posture when giving Reiki to oneself and others, as this assists your personal energy flow, as well as your general comfort, if treatments need to be given for extended periods of time. The most useful advice for the bodies' energy flow is to support this flow with an upright spine.

Conclusion

As you can see, there are many limiting beliefs surrounding Reiki and many which have been taken as gospel over the years. As part of our journey with Reiki, it is vitally important that we investigate information, even if it comes from our Reiki teacher and in this way, we can best determine if this suits us.

I call this spiritual self-reliance. In my classes, I often warn participants: *"Don't believe a word I am saying, I could be deluded and be leading you all astray. Check things out for yourself and find your way with Reiki"*

In our journey with Reiki, we all must be our own guiding lights and walk our path in the light of Reiki's truth.

To conclude, I would like to extend my sincere wish to you that by reading this volume, you can put some of this material to good use and benefit as many people as possible through your healing activity.

Yours in Reiki
Lawrence Ellyard

About the IIRT
The *International Institute for Reiki Training* offers traditional Reiki Training in a variety of styles and offers international training seminars for existing Reiki Practitioners and Masters, offering classes in Europe, the United Kingdom, The United States, Australia and New Zealand.

The IIRT also offers a Licensed Teacher Training Programme for existing Reiki Masters, who wish to establish a division of the IIRT in their country or capital city. For more information about the Institute visit: www.reikitraining.com.au

About the Author
Lawrence Ellyard has published four books on Reiki and has been a teacher of several Reiki traditions for more than twelve years. He

established the International Institute for Reiki Training in 1996 and has trained over 30 Reiki Masters. He currently teaches and lectures on Reiki throughout the world.

Recommended Reiki Websites

The Internet is a wealth of information, however, it is good to know where to go in that vast ocean. Following are a list of recommended websites, that cover an array of information about Reiki:

www.reikitraining.com.au *The International Institute for Reiki Training*
www.reiki.org *The International Centre for Reiki Training*
www.usui-do.org *Usui – Do*
www.reikialliance.com *The Reiki Alliance*
www.trtia.org *The Radiance Technique*
www.reiki.net.au *The International House of Reiki*
www.angelfire.com/az/SpiritMatters/contents.html *Reiki Ryoho Pages*
www.reikidharma.com *Reiki Site of Frank Arjava Petter*
www.angelreiki.nu *Reiki Plain and Simple*
www.threshold.ca *Reiki Threshold*
www.reiki-evolution.co.uk *Reiki Evolution*
www.healing-touch.co.uk *Healing Touch – Reiki Jin Kei Do*
www.australianreikiconnection.com.au *The Australian Reiki Connection*
http://reiki.7gen.com *The Reiki Page*
www.reiki-magazin.de *German Reiki Magazine*

Recommended Reiki Books

These titles presented here, are but a few of the more useful books that I have read on the subject.

Reiki Healer, A complete guide to the path and practice of Reiki – Lawrence Ellyard – Lotus Press
Reiki – Penelope Quest – Piatkus
Reiki – The healing touch – William Lee Rand – Vision Publications
Reiki – Way of the Heart – Walter Lubeck – Lotus Light
Reiki for First Aid – Walter Lubeck – Lotus Light
The Complete Reiki Handbook – Walter Lubeck – Lotus Light
Reiki Fire – Frank Arjava Petter – Lotus Light
Reiki – the Legacy of Dr. Usui Frank Arjava Petter – Lotus Light
The Original Reiki Handbook of Dr. Mikao Usui – Frank Arjaya Petter – Lotus Light

Reiki and the Seven Chakras – Richard Ellis – Vermillion
Modern Reiki Method for Healing – Hiroshi Doi – Fraser Journal
  Publishing
The Spirit of Reiki – A complete handbook of the Reiki System – Lotus
  Press.
Reiki for Beginners – David F. Vennells – Llewllyn
The Reiki Source Book – Frans and Bronwen Stiene – O-Books
  Publishing
Reiki – The essential guide to the ancient healing art – Chris & Penny
  Parkes – Vermillion
Empowerment through Reiki – Paula Horan – Lotus Light
Traditional Reiki – For Our Times – Amy Z. Rowland – Healing Arts
  Press

Contact Details

To find out more information about the International Institute for Reiki Training, including Reiki training and our Licensed Teacher Training Programme, visit: **www.reikitraining.com.au**

On our site, you will find over 100 pages on everything there is to know about Reiki. Our site is globally one of the most comprehensive and contains details on the Reiki styles and classes we offer, as well as Reiki history, Reiki news, Associate membership and details of where classes are held world-wide. The Institute also runs seminar tours in your country, so if you would like to learn with us, simply contact us from the site or write to us at:

The International Institute for Reiki Training
PO Box 548 Fremantle 6959 Western Australia
Phone: International +61 (8) 9335 1111

O

is a symbol of the world,
of oneness and unity. O Books
explores the many paths of wholeness
and spiritual understanding which
different traditions have developed down
the ages. It aims to bring this knowledge
in accessible form, to a general readership,
providing practical spirituality to today's seekers.

For the full list of over 200 titles covering:

- CHILDREN'S PRAYER, NOVELTY AND GIFT BOOKS
- CHILDREN'S CHRISTIAN AND SPIRITUALITY
- CHRISTMAS AND EASTER
- RELIGION/PHILOSOPHY
- SCHOOL TITLES
- ANGELS/CHANNELLING
- HEALING/MEDITATION
- SELF-HELP/RELATIONSHIPS
- ASTROLOGY/NUMEROLOGY
- SPIRITUAL ENQUIRY
- CHRISTIANITY, EVANGELICAL
  AND LIBERAL/RADICAL
- CURRENT AFFAIRS
- HISTORY/BIOGRAPHY
- INSPIRATIONAL/DEVOTIONAL
- WORLD RELIGIONS/INTERFAITH
- BIOGRAPHY AND FICTION
- BIBLE AND REFERENCE
- SCIENCE/PSYCHOLOGY

Please visit our website,
www.O-books.net